Better Homes and Gardens

calorie-smart meals

150 DELICIOUS DISHES WITH <300, <400, AND <500 CALORIES

HOUGHTON MIFFLIN HARCOURT
BOSTON · NEW YORK · 2015

Better Homes and Gardens® *Calorie-Smart Meals*

Editor: Jan Miller

Project Editor: Shelli McConnell, Purple Pear Publishing, Inc.

Contributing Editor: Ellen Boeke

Contributing Copy Editor and Proofreader: Terri Fredrickson, Gretchen Kauffman

Test Kitchen Director: Lynn Blanchard

Test Kitchen Product Supervisor: Carla Christian, R.D.

Test Kitchen Home Economists: Sarah Brekke, Linda Brewer, Juliana Hale, Sammy Mila, Jill Moberly, Colleen Weeden

Contributing Photographers: Karla Conrad, Jason Donnelly, Andy Lyons, Blaine Moats

Contributing Stylists: Greg Luna, Sue Mitchell, Dianna Nolin, Jennifer Peterson, Charlie Worthington

Administrative Assistants: Barb Allen, Marlene Todd

Special Interest Media

Editorial Leader: Doug Kouma

Editorial Director, Food: Jennifer Dorland Darling

Art Director: Gene Rauch

Houghton Mifflin Harcourt

Publisher: Natalie Chapman

Editorial Director: Cindy Kitchel

Executive Editor, Brands: Anne Ficklen

Editorial Associate: Molly Aronica

Managing Editor: Marina Padakis Lowry

Production Director: Tom Hyland

Waterbury Publications, Inc.

Design Director: Ken Carlson

Associate Design Director: Doug Samuelson

Production Assistant: Mindy Samuelson

Our seal assures you that every recipe in *Better Homes and Gardens® Calorie-Smart Meals* has been tested in the Better Homes and Gardens® Test Kitchen. This means that each recipe is practical and reliable and meets our high standards of taste appeal. We guarantee your satisfaction with this book for as long as you own it.

Pictured on front cover:
Chicken and Asparagus Skillet Supper, page 69
Pasta with Garlicky Steak and Red Onions, page 121
Citrus Salsa Salmon, page 169

Pictured on back cover:
Chicken and Lentils in Apple-Curry Sauce, page 224
Berry Tart with Lemon Cookie Crust, page 265
Pumpkin-Parmesan Risotto, page 184

Copyright © 2015 by Meredith Corporation, Des Moines, Iowa.

All rights reserved.

For information about permission to reproduce selections from this book, write to trade.permissions@hmhco.com or to Permissions, Houghton Mifflin Harcourt Publishing Company, 3 Park Avenue, 19th Floor, New York, New York 10016.

www.hmhco.com

Library of Congress Cataloging-in-Publication Data is available.

ISBN 978-0-544-56982-9 (pbk)
ISBN 978-0-544-56984-3 (ebk)

Book design by Waterbury Publications, Inc., Des Moines, Iowa.

Printed in the United State of America.

DOW 10 9 8 7 6 5 4 3 2 1
4500570463

smart meals

THE NUTRITION BREAKDOWN

Each recipe in this book is within a reasonable range of calories, fat, and sodium and with extra attention given to fiber and protein content.

Look for icons indicating that a recipe meets the following criteria:

☑ GLUTEN-FREE*
No ingredients contain gluten.

☑ MAKE-AHEAD
All or part of the recipe can be made in advance.

☑ HIGH-FIBER
Recipe contains 5 or more grams of fiber per serving.

☑ 30-MINUTE
Recipe can be ready in 30 minutes or less.

☑ VEGETARIAN
No ingredients contain meat or meat products.

*Gluten-free: These recipes can successfully be prepared with all gluten-free ingredients and may be suitable for people with celiac disease or other gluten sensitivities. Check the ingredient lists on all foods you use in these recipes to ensure they do not contain gluten.

You want a strong, healthy body, so you need to take care of it. A big part of that effort starts with how you fuel your body. *Calorie-Smart Meals* is loaded with thoughtful, tasty recipes that are nutritionally balanced so they do more than just meet your body's caloric needs.

Recipes are conveniently grouped by calorie level, giving you a simple tool for meal planning—with recipes for breakfast, lunch, and dinner in each level. In addition to main meals, you'll find nutritious snacks and delicious desserts under 250 calories. You'll also find basic information on important nutrients such as carbohydrate, fat, protein, and fiber to help you make good food choices throughout the week.

Your body only needs so many calories per day to function properly. The key to losing weight is to consume fewer calories and/or to exercise more to burn the extra calories you've consumed.

To get you started, we created two weeks of menu plans for you to use as a calorie-managing tool for balancing your calorie intake throughout the day and during the week. Use these menus as a guide to get you started on healthful eating habits for life.

contents

get smart, stay slim

DOES EATING WELL MAKE YOUR HEAD SPIN? WITH ALL THE LATEST RESEARCH AND NEW DIETS AVAILABLE, DECIDING WHAT TO EAT CAN BE OVERWHELMING. CUT THROUGH THE CONFUSION AND LEARN HOW TO EAT FOR OPTIMAL HEALTH. FROM CALORIES TO CARBS, BECOME OH-SO-SAVVY AT SELECTING THE HEALTHIEST FOODS.

What's in a Calorie?

If only we could eat unlimited amounts of everything and stay slim and healthy. Unfortunately, this is not reality. But you should remember: Calories are not the enemy—calories fuel the body.

You need to understand how calories affect your body and how to maximize your body's potential by eating the right ones. Don't simply count calories. Make the calories you eat count.

Where to start? Consider the following guidelines for figuring out how many calories your body needs. Once you settle into a healthy way of eating, you can adjust calories up or down to better meet your goals.

	Weight Loss Level	Weight Maintenance Level
Women	1,300–1,700 calories per day	1,600–2,000 calories per day
Men	1,700–2,000 calories per day	2,000–2,400 calories per day

Keep in mind calorie guidelines are simply that, GUIDELINES. Calorie needs will vary from person to person and can be affected by these factors: activity level, age, genetics, sleep, and stress level.

When it comes to weight loss, calorie quantity has been the gold standard for developing an eating plan. The number of calories you're eating is important. What's more important, however, is overall calorie quality. Our minds may crave unhealthy foods, but our bodies really crave the good stuff (such as whole fruits and vegetables, whole grains, lean meats and cheeses, beans and legumes, and nuts). Our bodies run more efficiently on healthy food, maintain a good weight more easily, and are better able to ward off conditions such as diabetes, digestive ailments, heart disease, and high blood pressure.

Losing weight does not mean you have to feel hungry and deprived. When you eat the right high-quality foods, you can eat robustly, feel satisfied from meals and snacks, and nourish your body with the nutrients it needs.

Calories in the foods we eat come from three main sources: carbohydrate, protein, and fat. Gram for gram, carbohydrate and protein contain the fewest calories (4 calories per gram of carbohydrate or protein); fat contains the most calories (9 calories per gram). Because fat has more calories by weight, it makes sense that avoiding fat altogether and eating only carbohydrates and protein would result in the quickest weight loss. Not so fast! Keep reading to see why not.

Carbohydrate Conundrum

You may have heard you shouldn't eat carbohydrates (aka carbs) if you want to lose weight. But with so many healthful foods in the carbohydrate family, following this advice is misguided. A wide variety of foods fits into the carbohydrate category, such as fruits, vegetables, grains, and sugar, and each one can be part of a healthful, slimming diet as long as you consume them wisely.

GOOD CARBS

Choose fruits, vegetables, and whole grains as the largest source of your carbohydrate foods throughout the day. Work toward reducing or eliminating your intake of added sugars, which are found in candy, soda, sugared cereals, cookies, and cake, not to mention indulgent coffee drinks. These foods provide little to no beneficial nutrients and can also produce big swings in blood sugar levels, which leaves you feeling groggy.

Make more room in your diet for high-quality carb foods, such as sweet potatoes, apples, whole grain pasta, broccoli, bananas, quinoa, carrots, and butternut squash. You will increase the amount of beneficial nutrients you take in and have more energy throughout the day.

Steer clear of low-quality carb foods like potato chips, apple juice, white bread, cookies, candy, white rice, soda, and energy drinks as much as possible. These tempting treats may give you an initial boost, but they will leave you feeling tired and sluggish.

BAD CARBS

Powerful Protein

Not only do protein-containing foods provide calories, their most important job is to furnish the building blocks needed to make, maintain, and repair major body parts such as muscle, bone, hair, and skin.

GOOD PROTEINS

Eating ample protein is the secret weapon to maximizing calorie intake and losing weight or maintaining a healthy weight. Protein helps you feel more full and satisfied, even if you are eating fewer calories. And high-protein foods "hold" you so you won't feel hungry long after eating your meal. Research shows that a high-protein breakfast helps keep you focused throughout the morning, which is a benefit anyone will like.

Protein exists in a variety of foods, but as with carb-containing foods, some are better than others. Choose the most-healthful protein foods, such as whole eggs, skinless turkey and chicken, fish and seafood, pork chops, beef sirloin, reduced-fat cheese, peanuts and natural peanut butter, Greek-style yogurt, lean ground turkey and beef, edamame, and cottage cheese.

Avoid low-quality protein foods like hot dogs, sausage, deli meat, processed cheese slices, bacon, corned beef, jarred cheese sauce, bologna, and fried chicken and fish. Most of these foods have added sugars and sodium.

BAD PROTEINS

Underrated Fat

We know how to calculate how many calories that fat provides the body, but many people underestimate the value of fat. This underappreciated nutrient deserves respect regarding weight loss and overall health.

GOOD FATS

There are two main types of fat in foods, saturated and unsaturated. A third type of fat, trans fat, is manufactured when unsaturated fat is processed into a saturated fat. Foods high in saturated and/or trans fats (butter and stick margarine; higher-fat cuts of beef, chicken, and pork; ice cream; packaged cookies; doughnuts; and fried foods) are more likely to contribute to negative health conditions such as heart disease, high blood pressure, cancer, and diabetes. Foods high in unsaturated fat can do the exact opposite, protecting the body from these conditions.

Healthy fats can be a dieter's strongest ally. Including healthy fats from avocados, nuts and nut butters, olive and canola oils, salmon and tuna, and seeds, such as flax, chia, and sesame, in meals and snacks helps maintain even blood sugar levels, which makes avoiding cravings throughout the day easier. Fat also helps the body absorb beneficial vitamins and antioxidants in food so that your body can actually use the good stuff you're eating.

BAD FATS

Fit and Fab with Fiber

With the focus on calories, carbs, and fat, we often forget fiber's importance in a healthful diet. The health benefits of fiber may not seem as crucial becuse it plays a supporting role to some of the more flashy components needed for optimal health.

Make sure fiber gets its due role in your diet. It helps control cholesterol, supports digestive health, and lowers the risk for heart disease, diabetes, and colon cancer. Fiber makes you feel full. You'll eat less later, which can impact weight loss tremendously. That's a hard-working nutrient!

Although fiber benefits the body in so many ways, American adults only consume on average 15 grams of fiber per day, which is much less than the recommended 25 to 35 grams.

Increase your consumption of the following high-fiber foods: flaxseeds, bran cereal, whole almonds, avocado, lentils, black beans, broccoli, quinoa, blackberries, and raisins, for example.

Power of Probiotics

It may seem that with all the food that passes through the gut (aka the small and large intestines), no one needs to worry about "feeding" the gut. That couldn't be more wrong!

We typically think of bacteria in a negative way, but the millions of bacteria in the gut can help or harm. "Good" bacteria are referred to as probiotics—they help keep harmful bacteria in their place. Probiotics are found naturally in the body as well as in fermented foods, such as yogurt, kefir, kombucha, tempeh, miso, sauerkraut, and even pickles. Eating foods with probiotics helps increase good bacteria in the gut. Prebiotics are found in beans and legumes, asparagus, oatmeal, and bananas to list a few. Prebiotics act as "food" to probiotics. They help foster an environment in the gut that promotes the production and maintenance of the probiotics. Research indicates that a gut full of healthy probiotics can help prevent eczema, allergies, and digestive issues, as well as promote healthy weight and boost the immune system.

cook smart

PROTEIN POWER

Studies have shown that adding protein to meals and snacks helps you feel full and satisfied longer, minimizing an attack of the munchies. Breakfast tends to be a carb-heavy meal, so try adding an egg, Greek yogurt, or a strip or two of lower-fat, lower-sodium bacon to boost the staying power of your meal. For snacks, a wedge of cheese gives you a quick and easy protein boost.

MEAL-PREP MUNCHIES

Ever feel like you've eaten half your meal before you even sit down? Snacking on ingredients while you cook can be a slippery slope. A bite here and a bite there as you make dinner can seem trivial until you add up the calories. Set a bowl of crunchy low-cal veggies on the counter for munching while you make your meal or chew a piece of gum to deter you from grabbing a bite of something else.

WISE SIDES

Side dishes may seem like innocent additions to a meal, but the calories and carbs can add up. Next time you need rice, try making cauliflower rice instead—finely chop fresh cauliflower in a food processor and steam it until tender. Swap cooked spaghetti squash for cooked pasta noodles or serve a stir-fry over wilted spinach or sautéed napa cabbage instead of higher-calorie, higher-carb noodles or rice.

PURGE YOUR PANTRY

Avoid buying tempting treats and snacks and start keeping your fridge and pantry full of healthy foods. If you're an ice cream junkie and can't stop until the carton is empty, it is better to not have any in the house. Instead, treat yourself to an occasional sundae from your favorite ice cream shop when you need a sweet fix.

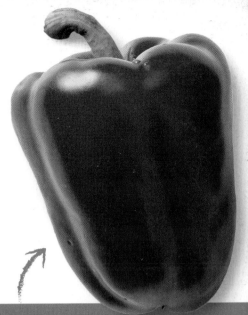

SEASONAL SUPERIORITY

Choosing in-season fruits and vegetables at peak ripeness means they taste better, and they'll have a higher concentration of beneficial vitamins and antioxidants. An added bonus: In-season produce tends to be more economical.

WHOLE AND FRESH ARE BEST

Whole, natural foods such as fresh fruits, vegetables, nuts, and unprocessed meats and cheeses are best for overall health as well as for weight loss. They contain more beneficial nutrients that the body thrives on and little of the additives and preservatives packaged, processed foods may contain.

FEAR FAT NO MORE

Some believe that to stay trim, you should avoid eating fat and fatty foods. In reality, moderate amounts of good fats (avocado, nuts, seeds, and fatty fish) can help you feel more satisfied and provide a host of health benefits, including lowered risk of heart disease and diabetes. Go ahead and drizzle olive oil on your salad, eat full-fat peanut butter, and chop some avocado for a fajita.

READ THE LABELS

Research shows that people who read nutrition labels tend to have a lower overall intake of calories, saturated fat, and sugar. Be wary of nutrition claims on the package, too. Just because a product claims to be healthy or low in "unhealthy nutrient X, Y, or Z," that doesn't mean it's a good choice. For example, a product claiming to be whole grain and healthy may be loaded with sugar or fat.

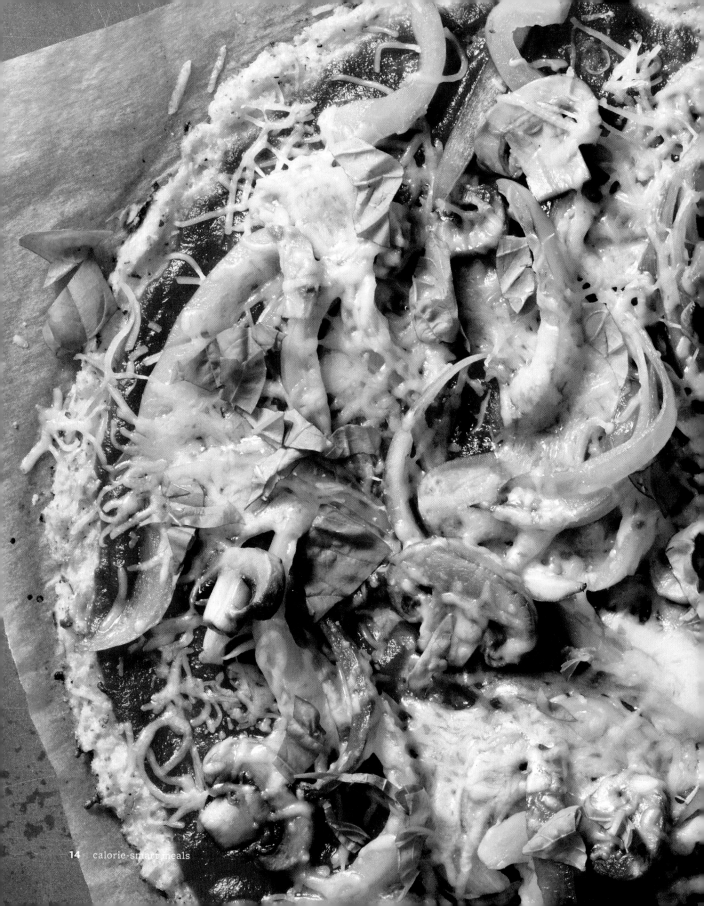

up to
300 calories

THESE RECIPES MAY BE SHORT ON CALORIES,
BUT THEY DON'T SKIMP ON SATISFACTION.
TURN TO THESE LEAN CHOICES WHEN
WEIGHT LOSS IS A PRIORITY.

mushroom, asparagus, and italian cheese omelets

Prep: 10 minutes   Cook: 20 minutes   Makes 4 servings (1 omelet each)

4	eggs, lightly beaten*
6	egg whites, lightly beaten*
¼	cup water
1	to 2 tablespoons finely snipped fresh Italian parsley or dill weed
	Dash salt
	Dash black pepper
2	tablespoons olive oil

1½	cups sliced fresh mushrooms
8	ounces fresh asparagus spears, trimmed and diagonally cut into 1-inch pieces
½	cup chopped red sweet pepper
½	cup sliced green onions
1	clove garlic, minced
¾	cup shredded reduced-fat Italian cheese blend (3 ounces)

1. In a large bowl combine the first six ingredients (through black pepper).

2. In a large nonstick skillet heat 2 teaspoons of the oil over medium-high heat. Add the next five ingredients (through garlic). Cook 5 to 8 minutes or until mushrooms begin to brown and asparagus is just tender, stirring frequently. Remove vegetables from skillet; cover and keep warm.

3. Heat a medium nonstick skillet with flared sides over medium-high heat until hot. Add 1 teaspoon of the oil, swirling to coat bottom of skillet. Add one-fourth of the egg mixture (about ½ cup); reduce heat to medium. Immediately stir egg mixture gently but continuously until mixture resembles small pieces of cooked egg surrounded by liquid egg. Stop stirring. Cook 30 to 60 seconds more or until egg mixture is set.

4. Spoon one-fourth of the vegetables onto half of the omelet. Sprinkle with one-fourth of the cheese. Lift and fold the unfilled half of the omelet over filling. Gently slide omelet out of skillet onto a warm plate. Cover and keep warm. Repeat with the remaining oil, egg mixture, vegetables, and cheese to make three more omelets.

*TIP: For a lighter version, substitute 2 cups refrigerated or frozen egg product, thawed, for the eggs and egg whites.

Per Serving: 247 cal., 15 g fat (5 g sat. fat), 197 mg chol., 362 mg sodium, 7 g carb., 3 g sugars, 2 g fiber, 21 g pro.

PERFECT PAIR   Serve a small bunch of fresh green grapes and a toasted whole grain English muffin half with each fluffy filled omelet.

confetti hash browns and eggs

Start to Finish: 30 minutes   Makes 4 servings (¾ cup hash browns and 1 egg each)

    2 teaspoons olive oil
    1 cup chopped onion
    2 cups chopped red, orange, green, and/or yellow sweet peppers
    1 cup finely chopped broccoli
 2½ cups frozen diced hash brown potatoes, thawed
    1 teaspoon snipped fresh thyme
    1 teaspoon Worcestershire sauce
  ½ teaspoon salt
  ¼ teaspoon black pepper
       Dash hot pepper sauce
    4 eggs

1. In a large nonstick skillet heat oil over medium heat. Add onion; cook 2 minutes. Add sweet peppers and broccoli; cook about 4 minutes or until vegetables are crisp-tender, stirring occasionally. Stir in the next six ingredients (through hot pepper sauce). Cook, covered, over medium heat about 12 minutes or just until potatoes are tender and golden, stirring occasionally.

2. Using a large spoon, make four indentations in potato mixture. Break an egg into each indentation. Cook, covered, 4 to 5 minutes more or until whites are completely set.

Per Serving: *240 cal., 8 g fat (2 g sat. fat), 186 mg chol., 417 mg sodium, 33 g carb., 4 g sugars, 4 g fiber, 11 g pro.*

PERFECT PAIR   A piece of whole grain toast with jam and a few orange slices on each plate complete this hearty breakfast.

three-cheese tomato tart

Prep: 40 minutes   Bake: 20 minutes at 400°F   Cool: 10 minutes   Makes 8 servings (1 wedge each)

½   of a 14.1-ounce package (1 crust) rolled refrigerated unbaked piecrust
Nonstick cooking spray

1   cup thinly sliced white or yellow onion

1   cup thinly sliced fennel

2   cloves garlic, minced

2   cups seeded and chopped tomatoes

½   teaspoon snipped fresh oregano or ¼ teaspoon dried oregano, crushed

¼   teaspoon salt

¼   teaspoon black pepper

¼   cup dried tomatoes (not oil-packed), finely snipped

1   tablespoon balsamic vinegar

1   egg

2   ounces reduced-fat cream cheese (Neufchâtel), softened

¾   cup shredded reduced-fat Jarlsberg cheese (3 ounces)

¼   cup thinly sliced green onions

¼   teaspoon crushed red pepper

½   cup grated Parmesan cheese

2   teaspoons all-purpose flour

2   medium tomatoes, sliced

1. Preheat oven and let piecrust stand according to package directions. Unroll piecrust into a 10-inch tart pan. Ease pastry into pan without stretching it. Press pastry into fluted sides of tart pan; trim edge. Bake according to package directions. Cool on a wire rack. Set oven temperature to 400°F.

2. Coat a medium skillet with cooking spray; heat skillet over medium-high heat. Add white onion and fennel to hot skillet; cook 5 minutes, stirring occasionally. Add garlic; cook and stir 1 minute more. Stir in the next four ingredients (through black pepper). Cook over medium heat about 10 minutes or until most of the liquid is evaporated. Remove from heat. Stir in dried tomatoes and vinegar; cool.

3. In a medium bowl combine egg and cream cheese until smooth. Stir in the next three ingredients (through red pepper). Reserve 1 tablespoon of the Parmesan cheese. Stir the remaining Parmesan cheese into cream cheese mixture.

4. To assemble tart, spread cooled tomato mixture in the bottom of baked tart shell; sprinkle with flour. Spread cheese mixture over tomato mixture to within ¼ inch of edge. Top with sliced tomatoes and the reserved 1 tablespoon Parmesan cheese.

5. Bake about 20 minutes or until golden. Cool on a wire rack 10 minutes. If desired, top with additional fresh oregano. Cut tart into wedges.

Per Serving: *214 cal., 11 g fat (5 g sat. fat), 37 mg chol., 327 mg sodium, 22 g carb., 4 g sugars, 2 g fiber, 9 g pro.*

PERFECT PAIR   Fresh peach slices drizzled with balsamic vinegar add a sweet note to this brunchworthy tart.

spicy sausage-sweet potato hash

Start to Finish: 30 minutes   Makes 2 servings (1 egg and 1 cup hash each)

- 1 small sweet potato, peeled and cut into ½-inch pieces (about 1 cup)
- ½ cup water
- ⅛ teaspoon salt
  Nonstick cooking spray
- 4 ounces uncooked turkey sausage links, chopped or crumbled
- ¼ cup chopped red onion
- 2 to 3 tablespoons water
- 1 teaspoon Worcestershire sauce
- 1 teaspoon balsamic vinegar
- ½ to 1 teaspoon sriracha sauce
- 2 eggs
  Snipped fresh Italian parsley and/or black pepper (optional)

SIMPLE SWAP

Opt for a splash of hot pepper sauce instead of parsley and pepper.

1. In a large skillet combine sweet potato, the ½ cup water, and salt. Bring to boiling; reduce heat. Simmer, covered, 5 to 8 minutes or just until tender. Drain.

2. Spray the same skillet with cooking spray. Add sausage; cook and stir over medium heat until browned. Stir in onion and the 2 to 3 tablespoons water, scraping up browned bits from bottom of skillet. Cook, covered, 2 minutes. Stir in the cooked sweet potato and the next three ingredients (through sriracha sauce). Cook and stir until potato is heated.

3. Using the back of a spoon, make two small indentations in the sweet potato mixture. Break an egg into each indentation. Cover and cook 2 to 3 minutes or until egg whites are set and yolks are starting to thicken. If desired, sprinkle with parsley and/or pepper.

Per Serving: 232 cal., 10 g fat (3 g sat. fat), 223 mg chol., 824 mg sodium, 18 g carb., 6 g sugars, 2 g fiber, 16 g pro.

farmer's casserole

Prep: 25 minutes   Bake: 40 minutes at 350°F   Stand: 5 minutes   Makes 6 servings (1 piece each)

Nonstick cooking spray
3 **cups frozen shredded hash brown potatoes**
¾ **cup shredded Monterey Jack cheese with jalapeño peppers or shredded cheddar cheese (3 ounces)**
1 cup chopped cooked ham
¼ **cup sliced green onions**
4 **eggs, beaten, or 1 cup refrigerated or frozen egg product, thawed**
1½ **cups milk or one 12-ounce can evaporated milk or evaporated fat-free milk**
⅛ **teaspoon salt**
⅛ **teaspoon black pepper**

SIMPLE SWAP

Use cooked breakfast sausage or Canadian-style bacon for the ham.

1. Preheat oven to 350°F. Coat a 2-quart square baking dish with cooking spray. Spread hash browns evenly in the dish. Sprinkle with cheese, ham, and green onions. In a bowl combine the remaining ingredients. Pour egg mixture over layers in dish.

2. Bake, uncovered, 40 to 45 minutes or until a knife inserted near the center comes out clean. Let stand 5 minutes before serving.

FARMER'S CASSEROLE FOR 12: Prepare as directed, except double all ingredients and use a 3-quart rectangular baking dish. Preheat oven to 350°F. Bake, uncovered, 45 to 55 minutes or until a knife inserted near the center comes out clean. Let stand 5 minutes before serving.

TO MAKE AHEAD: Prepare as directed through Step 1. Cover and chill up to 24 hours. Preheat oven to 350°F. Bake, uncovered, 50 to 55 minutes or until a knife inserted near the center comes out clean. Let stand 5 minutes before serving.

Per Serving: *263 cal., 12 g fat (6 g sat. fat), 175 mg chol., 589 mg sodium, 22 g carb., 3 g sugars, 2 g fiber, 17 g pro.*

squash, bacon, and feta breakfast bake

Prep: 35 minutes Bake: 1 hour at 375°F; 25 minutes at 350°F
Makes 6 servings (1 portion casserole and 1 egg each)

- 1 **3-pound spaghetti squash**
- ½ **cup refrigerated or frozen egg product, thawed, or 2 eggs, lightly beaten**
- ⅓ **cup finely shredded Parmesan cheese**
- 3 **tablespoons all-purpose flour**
- 2 **tablespoons snipped fresh sage**
- 6 **slices lower-sodium, less-fat bacon, coarsely chopped**
  Nonstick cooking spray
- 3 **cups coarsely chopped, trimmed Swiss chard**
- 2 **ounces reduced-fat feta cheese, crumbled (about ⅓ cup)**
- 6 **eggs**
- ¼ **teaspoon salt**
- ¼ **teaspoon black pepper**

SIMPLE SWAP

Fresh kale or spinach is a good stand-in for the chard.

1. Preheat oven to 375°F. Line a small baking pan with parchment paper. Cut spaghetti squash in half crosswise. Use a spoon to scoop out and discard seeds and strings. Place squash halves, cut sides down, on prepared baking pan. Bake about 1 hour or until squash is tender when pierced with a sharp knife. Cool completely on a wire rack. Reduce oven temperature to 350°F.

2. For crust, in a large bowl combine the next four ingredients (through sage). Using a fork, scrape squash pulp into the bowl with the egg mixture. Gently stir until well combined. Spread mixture in a greased 2-quart rectangular baking dish. Bake, uncovered, about 20 minutes or until crust is set and edges are starting to brown.

3. Meanwhile, in a large nonstick skillet cook bacon over medium heat until just browned but not crisp. Transfer bacon to a bowl. Drain and discard bacon drippings. Spray skillet with cooking spray. Add chard to skillet; cook and stir 1 minute.

4. Top squash crust with chard, feta cheese, and bacon. Bake, uncovered, about 5 minutes more or until heated through.

5. Coat the same skillet with cooking spray. Heat skillet over medium heat. Break three of the eggs into skillet, keeping eggs separate. Sprinkle with half of the salt and pepper. Reduce heat to low; cook eggs 3 to 4 minutes or until whites are completely set and yolks start to thicken. Remove from heat for sunny-side up eggs. For fried eggs over-easy or over-hard, when the whites are completely set and yolks start to thicken, turn eggs and cook 30 seconds more (for over-easy) or 1 minute more (for over-hard). Remove eggs from the skillet; keep warm. Repeat with remaining three eggs and remaining salt and pepper.

6. To serve, cut baked casserole into six portions. Serve each portion with an egg.

Per Serving: *213 cal., 10 g fat (4 g sat. fat), 195 mg chol., 549 mg sodium, 16 g carb., 5 g sugars, 3 g fiber, 16 g pro.*

bacon and egg muffins

Prep: 30 minutes   Bake: 15 minutes at 400°F   Cool: 5 minutes   Makes 12 servings (1 muffin each)

- 4 slices bacon, cut into thirds
- 5 eggs
- 2 tablespoons water
- Salt and black pepper
- 1 cup all-purpose flour
- ½ cup yellow cornmeal
- 2 tablespoons sugar
- 2½ teaspoons baking powder
- ½ teaspoon salt
- 1 cup milk
- ¼ cup vegetable oil or melted butter
- ½ cup shredded cheddar cheese (4 ounces)
- Maple syrup (optional)

1. Preheat oven to 400°F. In a large skillet cook bacon just until it begins to crisp. Drain bacon on paper towels. Reserve drippings. Return 2 teaspoons drippings to skillet. For scrambled eggs, in a bowl beat three of the eggs, the water, and a dash each salt and pepper. Cook eggs in hot skillet over medium heat, without stirring, until eggs begin to set on bottom and around edges. Lift and fold the partially cooked egg mixture so the uncooked portion flows underneath. Cook until egg mixture is cooked through but is still glossy and moist. Transfer to a bowl.

2. Brush twelve 2½-inch muffin cups with some of the remaining bacon drippings. In a medium bowl stir together the next five ingredients (through the ½ teaspoon salt). Make a well in center of flour mixture. In a separate bowl whisk together the milk, oil, and remaining two eggs. Add egg mixture all at once to flour mixture. Stir just until moistened (batter should be lumpy). Fold in scrambled eggs and cheese. Spoon batter into muffin cups (cups will be full). Place one bacon piece on each muffin.

3. Bake 15 to 17 minutes or until lightly browned and a toothpick inserted in centers comes out clean. Cool in cups on a wire rack 5 minutes. Run a small metal spatula or table knife around edges of muffins; remove from muffin cups. If desired, serve warm with maple syrup.

Per Serving: *202 cal., 12 g fat (3 g sat. fat), 89 mg chol., 356 mg sodium, 16 g carb., 3 g sugars, 1 g fiber, 7 g pro.*

PERFECT PAIR   Accompany these muffins with wedges of fresh cantaloupe and honeydew melon and whole strawberries.

salmon and quinoa cake benedict

Prep: 20 minutes   Stand: 20 minutes   Cook: 12 minutes
Makes 4 servings (1 quinoa patty, 1 egg, and toppers each)

- 3 egg whites, lightly beaten
- ½ cup soft bread crumbs
- ¼ cup grated Parmesan cheese
- 2 tablespoons chopped green onion
- ½ teaspoon bottled hot pepper sauce
- ¼ teaspoon salt
- 1¾ cups cooked quinoa*
  Nonstick cooking spray

- 3 tablespoons light sour cream
- 2 teaspoons Dijon-style mustard
  Fat-free milk (optional)
- 1 recipe Poached Eggs
- 2 ounces thinly sliced smoked salmon (lox-style)
  Cracked black pepper

1. In a bowl combine the first six ingredients (through salt). Stir in quinoa. Let stand 20 minutes. Form mixture into four 4-inch-diameter patties. Coat a large nonstick skillet with cooking spray. Heat skillet over medium heat. Cook patties about 3 minutes per side or until golden brown, turning once. Set aside and keep warm.

2. For sauce, in a bowl stir together sour cream and mustard. Thin with milk, if necessary, to reach desired consistency.

3. Prepare Poached Eggs. Top quinoa patties with smoked salmon, eggs, and sauce. Sprinkle with cracked black pepper and additional chopped green onions.

POACHED EGGS: In a large skillet combine 4 cups water and 1 tablespoon vinegar. Bring to boiling; reduce heat to simmering (bubbles should begin to break the surface of the water). Break an egg into a cup and slip egg into the simmering water. Repeat with three more eggs, allowing each egg an equal amount of space in the skillet. Simmer eggs, uncovered, 3 to 5 minutes or until the whites are completely set and yolks begin to thicken but are not hard. Using a slotted spoon, remove eggs from skillet. Season to taste with salt and black pepper.

*TIP: To make 1¾ cups cooked quinoa, in a small saucepan combine 1½ cups reduced-sodium chicken broth and ⅓ cup quinoa. Bring to boiling; reduce heat. Simmer, covered, about 15 minutes or until quinoa is tender. If necessary, drain off any excess liquid.

Per Serving: *210 cal., 9 g fat (3 g sat. fat), 200 mg chol., 866 mg sodium, 15 g carb., 1 g sugars, 1 g fiber, 18 g pro.*

PERFECT PAIR   Turn this brunch dish into a dinner entrée. Add a salad of torn fresh kale dressed with a balsamic vinaigrette and massaged until the leaves are tender and glossy. Top with slivered red onion and yellow sweet pepper.

strawberries and cream pancakes

Prep: 25 minutes   Cook: 2 minutes per batch

Makes 12 servings (2 pancakes, 1 tablespoon cream cheese, and ¼ cup strawberries each)

SIMPLE SWAP

Substitute sliced peaches or other fresh berries for the strawberries.

- 1 **orange**
- 3 **cups coarsely chopped fresh strawberries**
- 1 **cup whole wheat pastry flour**
- ½ **cup all-purpose flour**
- ¼ **cup oat flour or oat bran**
- 2 **tablespoons chia seeds or flaxseeds**
- 1 **tablespoon sugar**
- 1 **tablespoon baking powder**
- ¼ **teaspoon salt**
- 1½ **cups fat-free milk**
- ¼ **cup refrigerated or frozen egg product, thawed, or 1 egg, lightly beaten**
- 2 **tablespoons canola oil**
- ¾ **cup whipped Greek cream cheese,* softened**

1. Remove 1 tablespoon zest and squeeze ⅓ cup juice from orange. In a medium bowl combine strawberries, orange zest, and ¼ cup of the orange juice. Cover and let stand 20 minutes, stirring occasionally.

2. In a bowl stir together the next seven ingredients (through salt). Make a well in center of flour mixture. In another bowl use a fork to combine milk, egg, and oil. Add egg mixture all at once to flour mixture. Stir just until moistened (batter should be lumpy).

3. For each pancake, pour 2 tablespoons batter onto a hot lightly greased griddle or heavy skillet, spreading slightly. Cook over medium heat 1 to 2 minutes or until surface is bubbly and edges are slightly dry. Cook 1 to 2 minutes more or until browned. Keep pancakes warm in a 200°F oven while making the rest.

4. In a small bowl stir together cream cheese and the remaining orange juice; spread over pancakes. Top with strawberries.

*TIP: If you can't find whipped Greek cream cheese, use regular whipped cream cheese.

Per Serving: *158 cal., 5 g fat (1 g sat. fat), 6 mg chol., 236 mg sodium, 22 g carb., 7 g sugars, 3 g fiber, 6 g pro.*

179 CALORIES ☐ GLUTEN-FREE ☐ MAKE-AHEAD ☐ HIGH-FIBER ☑ 30-MINUTE ☑ VEGETARIAN

apple crisp hot cereal

Start to Finish: 10 minutes   Makes 1 serving (¾ cup)

½ cup hot cooked cereal (such as oatmeal)
¼ cup chopped apple
2 tablespoons low-fat granola without raisins
1 tablespoon chopped almonds
⅛ teaspoon apple pie spice

1. Place cooked cereal in a bowl. Top with apple, granola, and almonds. Sprinkle with apple pie spice.

Per Serving: *179 cal., 5 g fat (1 g sat. fat), 0 chol., 35 mg sodium, 29 g carb., 7 g sugars, 4 g fiber, 5 g pro.*

SIMPLE SWAP

Use ground cinnamon or ground nutmeg for the apple pie spice.

203 CALORIES ☐ GLUTEN-FREE ☑ MAKE-AHEAD ☑ HIGH-FIBER ☑ 30-MINUTE ☑ VEGETARIAN

good morning cereal blend

Start to Finish: 10 minutes   Makes 36 servings (¾ cup each)

8 cups whole-bran cereal
6 cups low-fat granola
4 cups wheat and barley nugget cereal (such as Grape Nuts brand)
7 cups seven-grain-and-sesame medley cereal (such as Kashi Medley brand)
2 cups dried cranberries and/or raisins
   Fat-free milk or yogurt (optional)

1. In a large bowl combine cereals and cranberries. If desired, serve with milk or yogurt.

TO STORE: Place cereal blend in an airtight container; cover. Store at room temperature up to 2 weeks or freeze up to 3 months.

Per Serving: *203 cal., 2 g fat (0 g sat. fat), 0 mg chol., 181 mg sodium, 48 g carb., 16 g sugars, 8 g fiber, 6 g pro.*

PERFECT PAIR   Serve this crunchy cereal blend with vanilla fat-free yogurt and a handful of fresh berries or cut-up peaches, plums, or bananas.

Apple Crisp Hot Cereal

overnight oatmeal with figs and yogurt

Prep: 10 minutes   Cook: 3 minutes   Stand: overnight   Makes 4 servings (¾ cup each)

- 3 **cups water**
- ¼ **teaspoon salt**
- 1 **cup steel-cut oats**
- ½ **cup unsweetened light coconut milk or almond milk**
- ½ **cup honey-flavor fat-free Greek yogurt**
- ¼ **cup snipped dried figs or dates**
- ¼ **cup sliced almonds, toasted**
- 2 **tablespoons shredded coconut, toasted**
- 4 **teaspoons honey**

SIMPLE SWAP

Change the flavors with a different yogurt, dried fruit, or nut.

1. In a medium saucepan bring the water and salt to boiling. Stir in oats; cover. Remove from heat; let stand overnight at room temperature.

2. In the morning, add coconut milk to oats. Heat over medium-low heat 3 to 5 minutes or until heated through, stirring occasionally. Top with the remaining ingredients.

Per Serving: *268 cal., 8 g fat (3 g sat. fat), 0 mg chol., 177 mg sodium, 44 g carb., 15 g sugars, 6 g fiber, 11 g pro.*

coconut chia oat bites

Prep: 20 minutes   Bake: 18 minutes at 325°F   Cool: 1 hour   Makes 6 servings (heaping ½ cup each)

Nonstick cooking spray
1 **cup rolled oats**
½ **cup oat bran**
½ **cup flaked or shredded coconut**
⅓ **cup packed brown sugar**
¼ **cup whole wheat flour**
3 tablespoons almond butter
2 **tablespoons water**
1 **tablespoon honey**
⅛ **teaspoon baking soda**
⅛ **teaspoon salt**
⅛ **teaspoon coconut extract**
2 **tablespoons chia seeds**

SIMPLE SWAP

No almond butter? Use peanut butter.

1. Preheat oven to 325°F. Coat a 15×10-inch baking pan with cooking spray. Place the next five ingredients (through flour) in a food processor. Cover and process until finely ground. Add the next six ingredients (through coconut extract). Cover and process until combined. Transfer mixture to a large bowl. Stir in chia seeds (mixture will be crumbly).

2. Using the bottom of a measuring cup, press oat mixture firmly into the prepared baking pan (mixture will be pressed thin). Bake 18 to 20 minutes or until golden brown. Cool in pan on a wire rack (mixture will crisp as it cools).

3. Use a table knife or small metal spatula to release the oat mixture from the pan. Break into small bite-size pieces (about ¾-inch pieces).

TO MAKE AHEAD: Place oat bites in an airtight container; cover. Store at room temperature up to 1 week.

Per Serving: *296 cal., 10 g fat (3 g sat. fat), 0 mg chol., 116 mg sodium, 48 g carb., 18 g sugars, 8 g fiber, 9 g pro.*

pineapple and yogurt breakfast sundaes

Start to Finish: 20 minutes   Makes 4 servings (¼ topped pineapple each)

1   whole medium fresh pineapple (about 3 pounds)
1   lime
1½   cups plain fat-free Greek yogurt
2   tablespoons honey
1   cup fresh raspberries and/or blackberries
¼   cup chopped toasted walnuts
2   tablespoons large flaked unsweetened coconut, toasted
     Finely chopped crytallized ginger, Chinese five-spice powder, or freshly grated nutmeg (optional)

SIMPLE SWAP

Sprinkle pineapple with pumpkin seeds (pepitas) or granola instead of walnuts.

1. Using a sharp knife, cut off top and bottom of pineapple; cut off peel. Quarter pineapple lengthwise. Cut core from each pineapple quarter. Slice fruit crosswise into ¼-inch-thick slices.

2. Remove ½ teaspoon zest and squeeze 2 teaspoons juice from lime. In a bowl stir together lime peel and juice, yogurt, and honey. Spoon yogurt mixture into bowls. Top with pineapple, berries, walnuts, and coconut. If desired, sprinkle with crystallized ginger, five-spice powder, or freshly grated nutmeg.

Per Serving: 244 cal., 6 g fat (1 g sat. fat), 0 mg chol., 42 mg sodium, 41 g carb., 32 g sugars, 5 g fiber, 12 g pro.

sloppy joe tostadas

Prep: 30 minutes   Bake: 7 minutes at 425°F   Makes 6 servings (1 tostada each)

- 8 ounces lean ground beef
- 8 ounces lean ground turkey
- 1 cup chopped, peeled sweet potato
- 1 14.5-ounce can no-salt-added diced fire-roasted tomatoes, undrained
- ½ cup water
- ½ of a 6-ounce can (⅓ cup) tomato paste
- 2 teaspoons hot chili powder
- 1 teaspoon cider vinegar
- ¼ teaspoon salt
- 6 6-inch corn tortillas
  Nonstick cooking spray
- 1 15-ounce can black beans, rinsed and drained
- ¼ cup crumbled queso fresco (1 ounce)
- 2 tablespoons snipped fresh cilantro (optional)

SIMPLE SWAP

Not into spicy? Pick a mild or medium chili powder.

1. Preheat oven to 425°F. In a large skillet cook ground beef, ground turkey, and sweet potato over medium heat until meat is browned. Drain off fat. Stir in the next six ingredients (through salt). Bring to boiling; reduce heat. Simmer, uncovered, about 10 minutes or until sweet potato is tender and mixture is desired consistency, stirring occasionally.

2. Meanwhile, place tortillas on a baking sheet. Coat both sides of tortillas with cooking spray. Bake about 7 minutes or until tortillas are crisp and starting to brown.

3. In a medium bowl coarsely mash beans just until they cling together. If necessary, add 1 to 2 tablespoons water to the beans to help mash. Microwave 1 to 2 minutes or until heated, stirring once. Spread mashed beans on tortillas. Top with meat mixture, queso fresco, and, if desired, cilantro.

Per Serving: *255 cal., 6 g fat (2 g sat. fat), 46 mg chol., 557 mg sodium, 28 g carb., 5 g sugars, 6 g fiber, 24 g pro.*

pho-flavor flank steak lettuce wraps

Prep: 30 minutes   Slow Cook: 5 hours (low) or 2½ hours (high)   Makes 6 servings (2 wraps each)

- 1   pound beef flank steak
- 2   cups coarsely chopped yellow onions
- 2   cups water
- ¼   cup fish sauce
- 2   tablespoons sugar
- 2   tablespoons rice vinegar
- 4   teaspoons Chinese five-spice powder
- 2   fresh jalapeño chile peppers, finely chopped*
- 12 large Boston lettuce leaves
- 4   ounces radishes, cut into thin bite-size strips (1 cup)
- ¾   cup fresh Thai basil leaves
- 3   green onions, thinly sliced diagonally
- 2   tablespoons lime juice
-     Sriracha sauce and/or lime wedges (optional)

SIMPLE SWAP

For a punch of vitamin K, use Swiss chard leaves in place of the Boston lettuce leaves.

1. Cut meat into 2-inch pieces. Place meat in a 3½- or 4-quart slow cooker. Top with yellow onions. In a bowl combine the next five ingredients (through five-spice powder) and half of the jalapeño peppers. Pour over mixture in cooker. Cover and cook on low for 5 to 6 hours or on high for 2½ to 3 hours.

2. Remove meat from cooker, reserving cooking liquid. Shred or chop meat; transfer to a bowl. Strain cooking liquid. Stir enough of the strained liquid (about ¼ cup) into shredded meat to moisten.

3. Divide shredded meat among lettuce leaves. Top with radishes, basil leaves, green onions, and the remaining jalapeño peppers. Sprinkle with lime juice. If desired, serve with sriracha sauce and/or lime wedges.

*TIP: Chile peppers contain oils that can irritate your skin and eyes. Wear plastic or rubber gloves when working with them.

TO MAKE AHEAD: Prepare as directed through Step 2. Let meat cool. Place in an airtight container; cover. Chill up to 3 days or freeze up to 3 months. Thaw if frozen. To reheat, warm meat in a Dutch oven over medium heat, stirring occasionally. Serve as directed.

Per Serving: 158 cal., 6 g fat (2 g sat. fat), 33 mg chol., 249 mg sodium, 9 g carb., 4 g sugars, 2 g fiber, 17 g pro.

greek beef kabobs with cucumber salad

Prep: 45 minutes   Grill: 10 minutes   Makes 4 servings (1 kabob and ¾ cup salad each)

- 2   tablespoons balsamic vinegar
- 2   teaspoons olive oil
- 2   teaspoons lemon zest
- 1   teaspoon dried oregano, crushed
- 2   cloves garlic, minced
- ¼   teaspoon salt
- ¼   teaspoon black pepper
- 1   pound boneless beef top sirloin steak
- 1   large red sweet pepper, seeded and cut into 1½-inch pieces
- 1   medium onion, halved crosswise and cut into wedges
- 1   recipe Cucumber Salad

1. In a shallow dish whisk together the first seven ingredients (through black pepper). Trim fat from meat. Cut meat into 1½-inch pieces. Add meat, sweet pepper, and onion to vinegar mixture; toss gently to coat. On four 10-inch metal skewers, alternately thread meat, sweet pepper, and onion.

2. Grill kabobs, covered, over medium heat 10 to 12 minutes or until meat is desired doneness, turning once. Serve kabobs with Cucumber Salad.

CUCUMBER SALAD: In a bowl stir together ½ cup plain fat-free Greek yogurt; 2 cloves garlic, minced; ½ teaspoon lemon zest; ½ teaspoon dried dill weed; ¼ teaspoon salt; and a dash cayenne pepper. Stir in 3 cups thinly sliced cucumber and ½ cup thinly slivered red onion.

Per Serving: 278 cal., 12 g fat (4 g sat. fat), 63 mg chol., 373 mg sodium, 12 g carb., 6 g sugars, 2 g fiber, 28 g pro.

PERFECT PAIR   Serve warm soft pita bread rounds with the kabobs and salad.

steak and cabbage salad with horseradish vinaigrette

Prep: 15 minutes   Grill: 12 minutes   Stand: 10 minutes
Makes 6 servings (1 cup salad and 2 ounces steak each)

- 1   **pound beef flank steak**
- 2   **tablespoons olive oil**
- 2   **tablespoons red wine vinegar**
- 1   **tablespoon prepared horseradish**
- 1   **teaspoon Dijon-style mustard**
- ½   **teaspoon black pepper**
- ¼   **teaspoon salt**
- 2   **tablespoons snipped fresh dill weed**
- 4   **cups coarsely chopped green cabbage**
- 1   **medium English cucumber, halved lengthwise and thinly sliced (2 cups)**
- 1   **large yellow sweet pepper, cut into bite-size strips**
- 1   **large red sweet pepper, cut into bite-size strips**

1. Grill steak, covered, over medium heat 12 to 17 minutes or until meat reaches desired doneness (145°F for medium rare; 160°F for medium), turning once. Transfer steak to a cutting board; cover with foil. Let stand 10 minutes.

2. For horseradish vinaigrette, in a screw-top jar combine the next six ingredients (through salt) and 1 tablespoon of the dill weed. Cover and shake well.

3. In a bowl combine the remaining ingredients. Drizzle with half of the vinaigrette; toss to coat. Transfer to a serving platter or divide evenly among plates. Thinly slice steak. Arrange steak on cabbage mixture. Sprinkle with the remaining 1 tablespoon dill weed and drizzle with the remaining vinaigrette.

Per Serving: *202 cal., 11 g fat (3 g sat. fat), 35 mg chol., 186 mg sodium, 8 g carb., 4 g sugars, 2 g fiber, 18 g pro.*

PERFECT PAIR   With this low-carb dinner, there's still room for bread. Brush slices of Italian bread with olive oil, sprinkle with finely shredded Parmesan cheese, and grill until cheese is melted.

delicata squash salad with pork medallions

Start to Finish: 30 minutes   Makes 4 servings (1 cup pork and squash mixture and 1½ cups spinach each)

12	ounces pork tenderloin, cut into ½-inch slices
¼	teaspoon salt
½	teaspoon black pepper
1	tablespoon olive oil
3	slices lower-sodium, less-fat bacon
1	pound delicata squash, seeds removed and cut into 1-inch pieces*
¾	cup unsweetened apple juice
¼	cup water
2	shallots, thinly sliced
3	tablespoons cider vinegar
1	teaspoon snipped fresh thyme or ¼ teaspoon dried thyme, crushed
6	cups fresh baby spinach

1. Sprinkle pork with salt and ¼ teaspoon of the pepper. In a large nonstick skillet cook pork in hot oil over medium-high heat about 5 minutes or until browned but still slightly pink in center, turning once. Remove from skillet; keep warm.

2. In the same skillet cook bacon over medium heat until crisp. Drain bacon on paper towels; crumble bacon. Wipe out skillet. Add the next four ingredients (through shallots) to skillet. Bring to boiling; reduce heat. Cook, covered, 6 to 8 minutes or until squash is just tender.

3. Add vinegar, thyme, and the remaining ¼ teaspoon pepper to skillet. Return pork and any accumulated juices to skillet; heat. Serve over spinach. Sprinkle with bacon.

*TIP: It is not necessary to peel delicata squash. The skin is tender after cooking and is a good source of fiber.

Per Serving: *226 cal., 6 g fat (1 g sat. fat), 58 mg chol., 315 mg sodium, 19 g carb., 5 g sugars, 4 g fiber, 22 g pro.*

PERFECT PAIR   Up the fiber with a side of hot cooked whole grain, such as quinoa, farro, or brown rice.

shredded pork roast sandwiches

Prep: 15 minutes   Roast: 2 hours 30 minutes at 325°F   Makes 12 servings (1 sandwich each)

1 **3-pound boneless pork shoulder blade roast**	½ **teaspoon black pepper**
8 **cloves garlic, minced**	½ **teaspoon cayenne pepper**
2 **teaspoons ground coriander**	2 **tablespoons vegetable oil**
2 **teaspoons ground cumin**	1 **cup beef broth**
2 **teaspoons dried oregano, crushed**	12 **hamburger buns or kaiser rolls, split and toasted***
1 **teaspoon onion powder**	**Barbecue sauce (optional)**
½ **teaspoon salt**	**Shredded cabbage (optional)**

1. Preheat oven to 325°F. Trim excess fat from meat. In a small bowl combine the next eight ingredients (through cayenne pepper). Sprinkle evenly over all sides of roast; rub in with your fingers. In a Dutch oven heat oil. Brown roast on all sides in hot oil.

2. Pour beef broth over roast. Cover and roast in oven 2½ to 3 hours or until very tender.

3. Using a slotted spatula or spoon, remove meat from cooking liquid. Skim excess fat from cooking liquid, reserving the liquid. When meat is cool enough to handle, shred meat using two forks. Stir enough of the cooking liquid into the shredded meat to moisten; reheat in a saucepan over medium heat. Serve on toasted buns. If desired, serve with barbecue sauce and/or shredded cabbage.

*TIP: To toast the buns, preheat broiler. Place split buns, cut sides up, on a broiler pan. Broil 4 to 5 inches from the heat about 1 minute or just until browned. Be sure to check the buns frequently to avoid burning.

SLOW COOKER DIRECTIONS: Prepare Shredded Pork Roast Sandwiches as directed in Step 1. Place roast in a 3½- to 5-quart slow cooker; add beef broth. Cover and cook on low for 8 to 10 hours or on high for 4 to 5 hours. Continue as directed in Step 3.

TO MAKE AHEAD: Prepare and shred meat as directed. Let meat cool. Place in an airtight container; cover. Chill up to 3 days or freeze up to 3 months. Thaw if frozen. To reheat, warm meat in a saucepan over medium heat, stirring occasionally. Serve as directed.

Per Serving: 295 cal., 10 g fat (3 g sat. fat), 68 mg chol., 461 mg sodium, 23 g carb., 3 g sugars, 1 g fiber, 26 g pro.

PERFECT PAIR   Add some reduced-fat coleslaw dressing to the shredded cabbage for a tangy go-with.

two-pea soup with pork

Prep: 30 minutes   Roast: 15 minutes at 425°F   Cook: 45 minutes   Makes 6 servings (1½ cups each)

2 medium carrots, cut into 1-inch pieces	½ teaspoon dried summer savory or marjoram, crushed
2 stalks celery, cut into 1-inch pieces	
1 large onion, cut into wedges	¼ teaspoon black pepper
3 cloves garlic, peeled	1 16-ounce package frozen green peas
1 tablespoon olive oil	⅓ cup packed fresh Italian parsley leaves
6 cups water	2 tablespoons lemon juice
2 pounds meaty smoked pork hocks	Salt
1 cup dried split peas, rinsed and drained	

1. Preheat oven to 425°F. In a shallow baking pan combine the first four ingredients (through garlic). Drizzle with oil; toss gently to coat. Spread vegetables in a single layer. Roast, uncovered, 15 to 20 minutes or until vegetables are lightly browned on edges, stirring once.

2. In a large Dutch oven combine roasted vegetables and the next five ingredients (through pepper). Bring to boiling; reduce heat. Simmer, covered, 45 minutes, stirring occasionally. Remove pork hocks; let cool slightly.

3. Stir frozen peas and parsley into Dutch oven; let cool slightly. Transfer vegetable mixture, half at a time, to a food processor or blender. Cover and process until nearly smooth. Return pureed mixture to Dutch oven. Stir in lemon juice.

4. When pork hocks are cool enough to handle, remove meat from bones, discarding bones. Coarsely shred enough of the meat to measure ¾ cup; set aside for garnish. Chop the remaining meat. Stir the chopped meat into Dutch oven. Cook soup over medium heat until hot.

5. Season to taste with salt and additional pepper. Top each serving with the reserved shredded meat.

TO MAKE AHEAD: Prepare as directed through Step 4. Transfer soup and the reserved shredded meat to separate airtight containers. Cover and chill up to 3 days or freeze up to 2 months. To serve, thaw soup and reserved meat if frozen. Transfer soup to a large Dutch oven. Cook over medium heat about 25 minutes or until heated, stirring occasionally. Continue as directed.

Per Serving: 267 cal., 5 g fat (1 g sat. fat), 25 mg chol., 663 mg sodium, 35 g carb., 9 g sugars, 13 g fiber, 21 g pro.

PERFECT PAIR   Serve with a slice of hearty rye bread to sop up every last drop of the delicious soup.

pork and poblano stew

Prep: 15 minutes   Cook: 24 minutes   Makes 4 servings (1½ cups each)

2	teaspoons hot chili powder
1¼	pounds pork tenderloin, cut into ¾- to 1-inch pieces
2	tablespoons olive oil
1	fresh poblano chile pepper, seeded and cut into 1-inch pieces*
1	large red sweet pepper, seeded and cut into 1-inch pieces
1	medium onion, cut into thin wedges
1	14.5-ounce can fire-roasted tomatoes with garlic, undrained
1	14.5-ounce can reduced-sodium chicken broth
3	inches stick cinnamon
1	orange

SIMPLE SWAP

Use plain diced tomatoes and a clove or two minced garlic if you can't find seasoned tomatoes.

1. In a medium bowl sprinkle chili powder over pork; toss to coat. In a large saucepan heat 1 tablespoon of the oil over medium-high heat. Add pork; cook about 4 minutes or until browned, stirring occasionally. Remove pork from pan.

2. Add remaining oil and the next three ingredients (through onion) to pan. Cook about 5 minutes or until vegetables are just tender, stirring occasionally. Add tomatoes, broth, and cinnamon stick. Bring to boiling; reduce heat. Simmer, covered, 10 minutes.

3. Meanwhile remove 2 teaspoons zest and squeeze ¼ cup juice from orange. Uncover saucepan; stir in reserved pork and the orange juice. Simmer 5 minutes more. Stir in orange zest. Remove and discard stick cinnamon before serving.

*TIP: Chile peppers contain oils that can irritate your skin and eyes. Wear plastic or rubber gloves when working with them.

TO MAKE AHEAD: Prepare as directed through Step 3. Let stew cool. Cover and chill up to 3 days. To reheat, bring stew to boiling. Serve as directed.

Per Serving: *300 cal., 11 g fat (2 g sat. fat), 87 mg chol., 534 mg sodium, 16 g carb., 8 g sugars, 4 g fiber, 32 g pro.*

lamb and bulgur burgers with dill-yogurt sauce

Prep: 20 minutes   Bake: 20 minutes at 350°F   Makes 6 servings (1 burger each)

- 1   6-ounce carton plain low-fat yogurt
- 2   teaspoons snipped fresh dill weed or ½ teaspoon dried dill weed
- ¾   cup water
- ½   cup bulgur
- ½   teaspoon salt
- ¼   cup finely chopped onion
- 3   tablespoons snipped fresh parsley
- 2   cloves garlic, minced
- 1   teaspoon ground coriander
- 1   teaspoon snipped fresh oregano or ¼ teaspoon dried thyme, crushed
- ⅛   teaspoon black pepper
- 12   ounces lean ground lamb
- 6   ciabatta rolls or whole wheat hamburger buns, split
     Tomato slices (optional)
- ½   of a medium cucumber, thinly sliced

SIMPLE SWAP

Not a fan of lamb? Ground turkey or lean ground pork is a great sub.

1. For sauce, in a small bowl stir together yogurt and dill weed. Cover and chill until ready to serve.

2. Preheat oven to 350°F. In a small saucepan bring the water to boiling. Stir in bulgur and ¼ teaspoon of the salt; reduce heat. Simmer, covered, 10 minutes. Remove from heat. Let stand, covered, 5 minutes.

3. In a bowl combine the remaining ¼ teaspoon salt and the next six ingredients (through pepper). Add cooked bulgur and ground lamb; mix well. Shape meat mixture into six ½-inch-thick patties. Place in a shallow baking pan. Bake 20 to 25 minutes or until done (160°F). Fill rolls with burgers, tomato slices (if desired), sliced cucumber, and sauce.

Per Serving: 295 cal., 11 g fat (4 g sat. fat), 40 mg chol., 454 mg sodium, 32 g carb., 5 g sugars, 4 g fiber, 18 g pro.

chicken thighs with caramelized onion and bacon dressing

Prep: 40 minutes   Cook: 31 minutes   Bake: 15 minutes at 400°F   Makes 4 servings (1 casserole each)

- 3 slices lower-sodium, less-fat bacon
- 3 large onions, halved and sliced (3 cups)
- 2 multigrain ciabatta rolls, cut into ½-inch cubes and dried*
- ½ cup reduced-sodium chicken broth
- ¼ cup refrigerated or frozen egg product, thawed, or 1 egg, lightly beaten
- 2 tablespoons snipped fresh parsley
- ¼ teaspoon black pepper
- 4 large skinless, boneless chicken thighs (about 1 pound)
- 1 tablespoon olive oil

SIMPLE SWAP

You can use any multigrain bread for the ciabatta rolls.

1. Preheat oven to 400°F. Cook bacon in a large skillet over medium heat about 10 minutes or until browned and crispy, turning once. Drain bacon on paper towels. Reserve 1 tablespoon of the bacon drippings in skillet. Add onions. Reduce heat to medium-low. Cook, covered, 13 to 15 minutes or until onions are tender, stirring occasionally. Uncover; cook and stir over medium-high heat 3 to 5 minutes or until golden. Remove from heat.

2. Chop the bacon. In a bowl stir together the bacon, caramelized onions, and the next five ingredients (through pepper). Divide dressing mixture among four individual 12- to 14-ounce casserole dishes.

3. In the same skillet cook the chicken in hot oil over medium heat about 5 minutes or until browned, turning once. Place one chicken thigh on dressing mixture in each casserole. Bake, uncovered, 15 to 20 minutes or until done (165°F). Before serving, sprinkle with additional snipped fresh parsley.

*TIP: To dry bread cubes, spread them in an even layer in a 15×10-inch baking pan. Bake in a 300°F oven 10 to 15 minutes or until cubes are dry, stirring twice; cool. (Cubes will continue to dry and crisp as they cool.) Or let bread cubes stand, loosely covered, at room temperature for 8 to 12 hours.

Per Serving: *288 cal., 9 g fat (2 g sat. fat), 110 mg chol., 357 mg sodium, 21 g carb., 5 g sugars, 3 g fiber, 28 g pro.*

peanut-ginger chicken wraps

Start to Finish: 20 minutes   Makes 4 servings (3 wraps each)

- **2** cups chopped cooked chicken breast
- **2** cups shredded cabbage with carrot (coleslaw mix)
- **1** medium carrot, cut up
- **2** green onions, cut up
- **2** tablespoons unsalted peanuts
- **1** teaspoon minced fresh ginger
- **⅓** cup light Asian salad dressing
- **⅓** cup drained canned crushed pineapple
- **12** leaves butterhead (Boston or Bibb) or green leaf lettuce

1. In a food processor combine about half of the first six ingredients (through ginger); cover and pulse several times until finely chopped. Transfer to a large bowl. Repeat with remaining half of the same ingredients. Add salad dressing and pineapple to mixture; stir to combine well.

2. Spoon about ¼ cup of the chicken mixture onto each lettuce leaf; roll up.

Per Serving: *221 cal., 8 g fat (2 g sat. fat), 60 mg chol., 267 mg sodium, 12 g carb., 8 g sugars, 2 g fiber, 24 g pro.*

PERFECT PAIR   Complete this light lunch with a carton of your favorite flavor of fat-free yogurt.

italian roasted chicken and vegetable toss

Prep: 25 minutes   Roast: 50 minutes at 375°F

Makes 6 servings (1⅓ cups greens and 1 cup chicken mixture each)

Nonstick cooking spray

2 bone-in chicken breast halves (about 2 pounds total)

1 cup peeled fresh baby carrots

1 medium onion, cut into 8 wedges

2 medium zucchini, cut into 1-inch chunks (about 3 cups)

1 medium red or green sweet pepper, cut into 1-inch chunks (about 1 cup)

8 ounces fresh mushrooms

3 tablespoons olive oil

¼ teaspoon salt

¼ teaspoon black pepper

2 tablespoons balsamic vinegar

1 teaspoon dried Italian seasoning, crushed

8 ounces Mediterranean blend salad greens (8 cups)

¼ cup shredded Parmesan cheese (1 ounce)

SIMPLE SWAP

Use any combination of torn fresh salad greens as a bed for this dish.

1. Preheat oven to 375°F. Coat a shallow roasting pan with cooking spray. Arrange chicken, skin sides up, in one half of the roasting pan. In the other half of the pan arrange the carrots and onion wedges. Roast, uncovered, 25 minutes.

2. Remove pan from oven. Add zucchini, sweet pepper, and mushrooms to the carrots and onion. Drizzle chicken and vegetables with 2 tablespoons of the oil and sprinkle with salt and black pepper.

3. Roast, uncovered, about 25 minutes more or until chicken is done (170°F) and vegetables are tender. Remove and set aside until cool enough to handle. Transfer vegetables to a bowl.

4. Remove and discard chicken skin and bones. Shred chicken using two forks. Add chicken and any juices in pan to vegetables; toss. In a bowl whisk together vinegar, the remaining 1 tablespoon olive oil, and the Italian seasoning. Add to chicken mixture; toss to coat.

5. Arrange salad greens on a platter or divide among six plates. Spoon chicken mixture over greens. Sprinkle with cheese.

Per Serving: 219 cal., 10 g fat (2 g sat. fat), 51 mg chol., 217 mg sodium, 10 g carb., 5 g sugars, 2 g fiber, 22 g pro.

parmesan-stuffed chicken and melted strawberries

Prep: 30 minutes   Bake: 15 minutes at 400°F

Makes 6 servings (1 chicken breast half and ½ cup strawberry mixture each)

- 3 **cups fresh strawberries***
- 2 **tablespoons white balsamic vinegar or white wine vinegar**
- ¼ **cup low-sugar strawberry preserves**
- ½ **teaspoon salt**
- ¼ **teaspoon black pepper**
- 6 **4- to 5-ounce skinless, boneless chicken breast halves**
- 2 **ounces Parmesan or white cheddar cheese**
- 6 **large fresh basil leaves**
- 2 **cloves garlic, minced**
- 1 **tablespoon olive oil**

1. Preheat oven to 400°F. In a 3-quart baking dish combine strawberries, vinegar, and preserves. Sprinkle with ¼ teaspoon of the salt and ⅛ teaspoon of the pepper.

2. Cut a horizontal pocket in each chicken breast half by cutting from one side almost to, but not through, opposite side. Cut cheese into six 3×½-inch pieces. Wrap a basil leaf around each piece of cheese; stuff into chicken breast pockets. Secure pockets with toothpicks. Sprinkle with the remaining ¼ teaspoon salt and ⅛ teaspoon pepper.

3. In an extra-large oven-going skillet cook garlic in hot oil over medium heat about 30 seconds. Add chicken; cook about 5 minutes or until golden brown, turning once. Transfer skillet with chicken to oven. Bake, uncovered, 5 minutes. Add baking dish with the strawberry mixture to oven. Bake 10 to 13 minutes or until chicken is done (165°F), berries are softened, and jam mixture has thickened. Serve chicken with melted strawberries.

*TIP: Halve or quarter any large strawberries before measuring.

Per Serving: *229 cal., 6 g fat (2 g sat. fat), 72 mg chol., 355 mg sodium, 11 g carb., 8 g sugars, 2 g fiber, 30 g pro.*

PERFECT PAIR   Accompany this sweet-tart dish with hot cooked whole grain pasta or quinoa.

orange chicken thighs with cauliflower rice

Prep: 25 minutes   Bake: 30 minutes at 375°F   Cook: 18 minutes

Makes 4 servings (1 chicken thigh and ⅓ cup cauliflower rice each)

	Nonstick cooking spray
2	tablespoons sesame oil (not toasted)
4	large bone-in chicken thighs (about 2¼ pounds total), skin removed
1	orange
1	tablespoon reduced-sodium soy sauce
1	tablespoon rice vinegar
1	tablespoon packed brown sugar
1	teaspoon cornstarch
¼	teaspoon crushed red pepper
4	cups coarsely chopped cauliflower florets
½	teaspoon kosher salt
⅛	teaspoon black pepper
	Snipped fresh cilantro (optional)

SIMPLE SWAP

Go beyond white cauliflower. Try an orange, green, or even purple variety.

1. Preheat oven to 375°F. Coat a 2-quart square baking dish with cooking spray. In an extra-large nonstick skillet heat 1 tablespoon of the sesame oil over medium-high heat. Add chicken thighs; cook about 10 minutes or until browned, turning once. Transfer chicken to prepared dish. Wipe out skillet.

2. Remove 1 teaspoon zest and squeeze 1 tablespoon juice from orange. (If desired, set aside additional zest for garnish.) In a small bowl whisk together zest, juice, 2 tablespoons cold water, and the next five ingredients (through red pepper); add to the skillet. Cook and stir until thickened and bubbly; pour over chicken thighs. Bake, uncovered, about 30 minutes or until chicken is done (at least 175°F).

3. Meanwhile, place cauliflower in a large food processor. Cover and pulse several times until cauliflower is evenly chopped into rice-size pieces.

4. Heat the remaining 1 tablespoon oil in the skillet over medium-high heat; add cauliflower, salt, and pepper. Cook 8 to 10 minutes or until you begin to see caramelized flecks throughout cauliflower, stirring occasionally. If desired, sprinkle cauliflower with cilantro and additional orange zest. Serve with chicken thighs.

Per Serving: *285 cal., 13 g fat (3 g sat. fat), 145 mg chol., 526 mg sodium, 9 g carb., 5 g sugars, 2 g fiber, 32 g pro.*

chicken with apple-vegetable slaw stir-fry

Start to Finish: 40 minutes   Makes 4 servings (1½ cups each)

½ cup reduced-sodium chicken broth
2 tablespoons cider vinegar
1 tablespoon packed brown sugar
2 teaspoons Dijon-style mustard
2 teaspoons cornstarch
1 clove garlic, minced
½ teaspoon crushed red pepper
½ teaspoon salt
2 tablespoons vegetable oil

12 ounces boneless, skinless chicken thighs, cut into bite-size pieces
2 cups quartered fresh cremini mushrooms
¼ cup sliced shallots
3 cups coarsley shredded green cabbage
8 ounces fresh asparagus spears, trimmed and cut into 2-inch pieces
1 medium tart apple, cored and thinly sliced
Snipped fresh cilantro

1. For sauce, in a bowl stir together the first eight ingredients (through salt).

2. In a wok or very large skillet heat 1 tablespoon of the oil over medium-high heat. Add chicken; cook and stir 4 to 6 minutes or until chicken is no longer pink. Transfer to a bowl. Heat the remaining 1 tablespoon oil in skillet. Add mushrooms and shallots; cook and stir 2 to 3 minutes. Add cabbage, asparagus, and apple; cook and stir 3 to 5 minutes more or until vegetables are crisp-tender.

3. Push vegetables to side of wok. Stir sauce; add to center of wok. Cook and stir until thickened and bubbly. Return chicken to wok. Cook and stir 1 minute more. Sprinkle with cilantro.

Per Serving: *247 cal., 11 g fat (2 g sat. fat), 80 mg chol., 514 mg sodium, 19 g carb., 12 g sugars, 4 g fiber, 20 g pro.*

PERFECT PAIR   This stir-fry is not a typical Asian stir-fry. It can be served with hot cooked brown rice, but oven-fried potatoes are equally as good.

chicken and asparagus skillet supper

Start to Finish: 35 minutes   Makes 4 servings (1 chicken breast half and ¾ cup vegetables each)

1   **pound asparagus spears, trimmed**
4   **slices bacon, coarsely chopped**
4   **skinless, boneless chicken breast halves**
     Salt and black pepper
1   **yellow summer squash, halved lengthwise and cut into ½-inch pieces**
1   **14.5-ounce can reduced-sodium chicken broth***
2   **tablespoons all-purpose flour**
½   **teaspoon lemon zest**
     Lemon wedges

1. In a large saucepan cook asparagus in boiling water about 3 minutes or until crisp-tender; drain. Immediately plunge asparagus into ice water to stop cooking; drain.

2. In an extra-large skillet cook bacon over medium heat until crisp. Drain bacon on paper towels. Reserve 1 tablespoon of the drippings in skillet. Discard remaining drippings.

3. Lightly sprinkle chicken with salt and pepper. Cook chicken in hot drippings over medium-high heat about 12 minutes or until browned, turning once. Remove chicken from skillet; keep warm.

4. Add squash to skillet; cook 3 minutes. In a bowl whisk together broth, flour, and lemon zest; add to skillet. Cook and stir until thickened and bubbly. Add chicken and asparagus to skillet. Cook about 6 minutes more or until chicken is done (165°F). Sprinkle with bacon. Serve with lemon wedges.

*TIP: Or use 1½ cups chicken broth and ¼ cup dry white wine.

Per Serving: *238 cal., 9 g fat (3 g sat. fat), 82 mg chol., 630 mg sodium, 8 g carb., 2 g sugars, 2 g fiber, 30 g pro.*

PERFECT PAIR   Toss together baby kale, thinly sliced red onion, halved grape tomatoes, a sprinkling of sunflower kernels, and a light Caesar dressing to serve on the side.

smoky chicken tortilla soup

Start to Finish: 30 minutes   Makes 6 servings (1⅔ cups each)

- 1 **tablespoon vegetable oil**
- 1 **cup chopped onion**
- 1 **teaspoon ground cumin**
- 1 **32-ounce carton reduced-sodium chicken broth**
- 2 **14.5-ounce cans no-salt-added fire-roasted diced tomatoes, undrained**
- 1½ **cups coarsely shredded cooked chicken breast**
- 1½ **cups frozen whole kernel corn**
- 2 **4-ounce cans diced green chile peppers, undrained**
- 2 **cups coarsely crushed tortilla chips**
- ½ **cup snipped fresh cilantro**
- ½ **cup shredded Monterey Jack cheese (2 ounces) (optional)**
  Lime wedges (optional)

SIMPLE SWAP

Top this soup with Monterey Jack cheese with jalapeño peppers for a little more zip.

1. In a 4-quart Dutch oven heat oil over medium heat. Add onion and cumin; cook about 5 minutes or until onion is tender, stirring frequently. Add the next five ingredients (through chile peppers). Bring to boiling; reduce heat. Simmer, covered, 10 minutes.

2. Divide crushed tortilla chips among soup bowls. Top with soup and cilantro. If desired, sprinkle with cheese and/or serve with lime wedges.

TO MAKE AHEAD: Prepare as directed through Step 1. Let soup cool. Cover and chill up to 3 days. To reheat, bring soup to boiling. Serve as directed.

Per Serving: *280 cal., 10 g fat (2 g sat. fat), 29 mg chol., 579 mg sodium, 31 g carb., 6 g sugars, 4 g fiber, 17 g pro.*

lentil-toasted barley soup with sausage

Prep: 35 minutes   Cook: 55 minutes   Makes 6 servings (1⅓ cups each)

- 1 tablespoon olive oil
- ½ cup regular barley
- 1 cup chopped onion
- ¾ cup chopped carrots
- 2 cloves garlic, minced
- 2 teaspoons ground cumin
- 4 cups reduced-sodium chicken broth
- 1 cup water
- ½ cup lentils, rinsed and drained
- 1 bay leaf
- 1 14.5-ounce can no-salt-added diced fire-roasted tomatoes, undrained
- 6 ounces cooked chicken-apple sausage links, halved lengthwise and sliced
- 4 cups fresh baby spinach

1. In a 3- to 4-quart saucepan heat oil over medium heat. Add barley; cook and stir 3 to 4 minutes or until barley is golden. Add onion, carrots, and garlic; cook about 10 minutes or just until vegetables are tender, stirring occasionally. Stir in cumin; cook and stir 30 seconds more.

2. Add the next four ingredients (through bay leaf). Bring to boiling; reduce heat. Simmer, covered, about 55 minutes or until barley and lentils are tender. Stir in tomatoes and sausage; heat. Remove and discard bay leaf. Add spinach, stirring until spinach begins to wilt. Serve immediately.

TO MAKE AHEAD: Prepare as directed through Step 2, except do not add spinach. Let soup cool. Cover and chill up to 3 days. To reheat, bring stew to boiling. Continue as directed.

Per Serving: *245 cal., 7 g fat (2 g sat. fat), 32 mg chol., 645 mg sodium, 33 g carb., 5 g sugars, 10 g fiber, 14 g pro.*

PERFECT PAIR   Sliced apples and wedges of cheddar cheese can serve as salad or dessert with this hearty meal.

salmon in parchment paper

Prep: 30 minutes   Bake: 25 minutes at 350°F   Makes 4 servings (1 packet each)

- 1 pound fresh or frozen skinless salmon or halibut fillets, ¾ to 1 inch thick
- 4 cups fresh vegetables (such as sliced carrots,* trimmed fresh green beans,* sliced zucchini or yellow summer squash, sliced fresh mushrooms, and/or sliced red, yellow, and/or green sweet peppers)
- ½ cup sliced green onions
- 1 tablespoon snipped fresh oregano or 1 teaspoon dried oregano, crushed
- 2 teaspoons orange zest
- ¼ teaspoon salt
- ¼ teaspoon black pepper
- 4 cloves garlic, halved
- 4 teaspoons olive oil
- 1 medium orange, halved and thinly sliced
- 4 sprigs fresh oregano (optional)

SIMPLE SWAP

Lemon zest and slices are a zippy trade for the orange zest and slices.

1. Preheat oven to 350°F. Thaw fish, if frozen. Rinse fish; pat dry with paper towels. If necessary, cut into four serving-size pieces. Tear off four 14-inch squares of parchment paper. In a large bowl combine the next seven ingredients (through garlic); toss gently.

2. Divide vegetable mixture among the four pieces of parchment, placing vegetables on one side of each parchment square. Place one fish piece on top of each vegetable portion. Drizzle 1 teaspoon of the oil over each fish piece. Sprinkle lightly with additional salt and black pepper; top with orange slices. Fold parchment over fish and vegetables; fold in the open sides several times to secure, curving the edge into a circular pattern. Place parchment packets in a single layer in a 15×10-inch baking pan.

3. Bake 25 to 30 minutes or until fish flakes easily. Cut an "X" in the top of a parchment packet to check doneness; open carefully (steam will escape). If desired, garnish with fresh oregano sprigs.

*TIP: If using carrots and/or green beans, precook them. In a covered medium saucepan cook the carrots and/or green beans in a small amount of boiling water 2 minutes. Drain.

Per Serving: *262 cal., 12 g fat (2 g sat. fat), 62 mg chol., 359 mg sodium, 13 g carb., 8 g sugars, 4 g fiber, 25 g pro.*

roasted salmon with tomatoes and corn

Prep: 25 minutes   Roast: 15 minutes at 400°F

Makes 4 servings (3 ounces salmon and ½ cup vegetable mixture each)

1	1-pound fresh or frozen salmon fillet, skinned if desired
	Nonstick cooking spray
½	teaspoon salt
½	teaspoon black pepper
2	cups halved grape or cherry tomatoes
2	cups frozen or fresh whole kernel corn
2	teaspoons olive oil
1	teaspoon chili powder
½	teaspoon ground cumin
1	lime
1	tablespoon lime juice
1	teaspoon honey
¼	cup finely chopped red onion
2	tablespoons snipped fresh cilantro
	Fresh cilantro leaves

1. Thaw salmon, if frozen. Rinse fish and pat dry with paper towels. Preheat oven to 400°F. Line a 15×10-inch baking pan with foil; coat foil with cooking spray. Place salmon in prepared pan. Sprinkle with ¼ teaspoon each of the salt and pepper.

2. In a bowl combine the next five ingredients (through cumin) and the remaining salt and pepper. Toss to coat. Spread tomato mixture around salmon in pan. Roast, uncovered, 15 to 18 minutes or until fish flakes easily.

3. Meanwhile, remove ½ teaspoon zest and squeeze 1 tablespoon juice from lime. In a bowl stir together lime zest, lime juice, and honey.

4. Transfer salmon to a platter. Brush salmon with honey mixture. Add onion and snipped cilantro to tomatoes in pan; stir gently to combine. Top salmon with tomato mixture and cilantro leaves.

Per Serving: *285 cal., 11 g fat (2 g sat. fat), 62 mg chol., 360 mg sodium, 24 g carb., 6 g sugars, 3 g fiber, 26 g pro.*

PERFECT PAIR   Serve this colorful dish with a crisp green salad topped with thin apple slices, toasted walnuts, and a light balsamic vinaigrette.

salmon-stuffed zucchini

Prep: 25 minutes   Broil: 7 minutes   Makes 4 servings (2 zucchini halves each)

- 4 **medium zucchini (about 8 ounces each)**
- ⅓ **cup finely chopped green onions**
- ¼ **cup bottled roasted red sweet pepper, drained and chopped**
- ¼ **cup light mayonnaise**
- 2 **tablespoons snipped fresh parsley**
- 1 **teaspoon dried Italian seasoning, crushed**
- 3 **2.5-ounce pouches lemon-pepper or plain skinless, boneless pink salmon**
- ½ **cup panko bread crumbs**
- ½ **cup finely shredded Gruyere or Parmesan cheese (2 ounces)**
  Lemon wedges

1. Preheat broiler. Trim ends of zucchini if desired; cut each zucchini in half lengthwise. Using a melon baller or a small spoon, scoop out and discard pulp, leaving ¼-inch-thick shells. Place zucchini shells, cut sides up, in a shallow baking pan. Broil 4 inches from the heat 4 to 5 minutes or until edges of zucchini start to brown.

2. Meanwhile, in a bowl stir together the next five ingredients (through Italian seasoning). Add salmon and bread crumbs. Stir gently to combine.

3. Spoon salmon mixture into broiled zucchini halves. Sprinkle with cheese. Broil about 3 minutes or until cheese is melted and golden. Serve with lemon wedges.

Per Serving: *228 cal., 11 g fat (4 g sat. fat), 40 mg chol., 558 mg sodium, 16 g carb., 8 g sugars, 3 g fiber, 19 g pro.*

PERFECT PAIR   Serve stuffed zucchini with hot cooked risotto or polenta. For more color, stir in shredded fresh spinach and/or very thin sweet pepper strips.

tuna and hummus wraps

Start to Finish: 20 minutes   Makes 4 servings (1 wrap each)

1	6-ounce can very low-sodium chunk white tuna (water pack), drained
1½	cups peeled, seeded, and finely chopped cucumber
½	cup seeded and chopped tomato
2	tablespoons olive oil
1	tablespoon snipped fresh dill weed or 1 teaspoon dried dill weed
¼	teaspoon black pepper
4	cups torn packaged lettuce, such as hearts of romaine, European blend, or Mediterranean blend
4	7- to 8-inch whole wheat flour tortillas
⅓	cup cucumber-dill hummus

1. In a bowl stir together the first six ingredients (through pepper). Add torn lettuce; toss to combine. Spread tortillas with hummus. Top with tuna mixture. Roll up tortillas and, if necessary, secure with toothpicks.

Per Serving: *280 cal., 11 g fat (1 g sat. fat), 19 mg chol., 482 mg sodium, 32 g carb., 2 g sugars, 4 g fiber, 16 g pro.*

PERFECT PAIR   A wedge or two of fresh melon is an ideal side with this lunchtime sandwich.

almond-crusted mahi mahi with lemon wine sauce

Prep: 25 minutes   Bake: 4 minutes at 450°F   Makes 4 servings (1 fillet and 2 tablespoons sauce each)

SIMPLE SWAP

Any firm white fish, such as halibut, can be used for mahi mahi.

Nonstick cooking spray

4 4- to 5-ounce fresh or frozen mahi mahi fillets

1 egg white, lightly beaten

1 tablespoon water

⅓ cup sliced almonds, coarsely broken

2 tablespoons fine dry bread crumbs

1 tablespoon snipped fresh thyme

¼ teaspoon salt

1 tablespoon light butter with canola oil

1 tablespoon finely chopped shallots

1½ teaspoons all-purpose flour

⅛ teaspoon salt

Dash black pepper

½ cup dry white wine, such as Chardonnay

1 tablespoon lemon juice

½ teaspoon snipped fresh thyme

1. Preheat oven to 450°F. Line a baking sheet with foil. Coat foil with cooking spray. Thaw fish, if frozen. Rinse fish; pat dry with paper towels. Measure thickness of fish.

2. In a shallow dish combine egg white and the water. In a second shallow dish combine the next four ingredients (through ¼ teaspoon salt). Dip fillets in egg white mixture, turning to coat. Dip in almond mixture, turning to coat evenly.

3. Place fish on the prepared baking sheet. Sprinkle any remaining almond mixture over fish. Coat fish with cooking spray. Bake 4 to 6 minutes per ½-inch thickness or until fish flakes easily.

4. Meanwhile, in a small saucepan melt butter over medium heat. Add shallots; cook 3 minutes, stirring occasionally. Add the next three ingredients (through pepper), stirring until flour is coated. Add wine and lemon juice all at once. Cook and stir until thickened and bubbly. Cook and stir 1 minute more. Remove from heat. Stir in the ½ teaspoon thyme. Drizzle sauce over fish. If desired, top with additional snipped fresh thyme.

Per Serving: *203 cal., 6 g fat (1 g sat. fat), 84 mg chol., 383 mg sodium, 6 g carb., 1 g sugars, 1 g fiber, 24 g pro.*

lemon shrimp with spinach quinoa

Start to Finish: 30 minutes   Makes 4 servings (½ cup shrimp mixture and ½ cup quinoa each)

1 **pound fresh or frozen large shrimp in shells**	2 **tablespoons lemon juice**
1 **recipe Spinach Quinoa**	⅛ **teaspoon black pepper**
1 **teaspoon all-purpose flour**	1 **tablespoon unsalted butter**
⅓ **cup dry white wine or ¼ cup reduced-sodium chicken broth plus 1 tablesoon white wine vinegar**	½ **cup thinly sliced red onion** **Lemon wedges (optional)**

1. Thaw shrimp, if frozen. Prepare Spinach Quinoa. Meanwhile, peel and devein shrimp, leaving tails intact if desired. Rinse shrimp; pat dry with paper towels. Place shrimp in a bowl. Sprinkle with flour; toss to coat. For sauce, in a bowl stir together wine, lemon juice, and pepper.

2. In a large skillet melt butter over medium-high. Add onion; cook about 5 minutes or until tender, stirring occasionally. Add shrimp; cook and stir 1 to 2 minutes or until shrimp start to turn opaque. Carefully add sauce; bring to boiling. Cook and stir about 1 minute more or until shrimp are opaque and sauce is thickened.

3. Spoon shrimp mixture over Spinach Quinoa. If desired, serve with lemon wedges.

SPINACH QUINOA: In a small saucepan combine 1 cup water; ½ cup red or regular quinoa; 1 clove garlic, minced; and ¼ teaspoon salt. Bring to boiling; reduce heat. Simmer, covered, about 15 minutes or until liquid is absorbed. Stir in 2 cups fresh baby spinach and ½ teaspoon lemon zest.

Per Serving: *227 cal., 6 g fat (2 g sat. fat), 137 mg chol., 287 mg sodium, 19 g carb., 1 g sugars, 2 g fiber, 21 g pro.*

PERFECT PAIR   Enjoy lemon sorbet garnished with fresh mint for a sweet-tart dessert.

baked shrimp and rice

Prep: 30 minutes   Bake: 30 minutes at 350°F   Makes 6 servings (¾ cup each)

- **12** **ounces fresh or frozen peeled and deveined cooked shrimp**
- **2** **tablespoons butter**
- **½** **cup chopped onion**
- **¼** **cup chopped green or red sweet pepper**
- **2** **cups cooked white rice**
- **1** **10.75-ounce can condensed cream of shrimp or cream of celery soup**
- **½** **cup half-and-half**
- **2** **tablespoons dry sherry**
- **1** **teaspoon lemon juice**
- **¼** **teaspoon salt**
- **⅛** **teaspoon cayenne pepper**
- **3** **tablespoons sliced almonds, toasted**
- **Snipped fresh cilantro**

SIMPLE SWAP

Bump up the fiber with brown rice.

1. Thaw shrimp, if frozen. Rinse shrimp; pat dry with paper towels. Preheat oven to 350°F. In a large saucepan melt butter over medium heat. Add onion and sweet pepper; cook until tender, stirring occasionally. Remove from heat.

2. Stir shrimp and the next seven ingredients (through cayenne pepper) into vegetable mixture. Transfer to a 1½-quart square baking dish. Bake, uncovered, about 30 minutes or until heated. Sprinkle with almonds and cilantro.

Per Serving: *290 cal., 13 g fat (5 g sat. fat), 141 mg chol., 624 mg sodium, 23 g carb., 1 g sugars, 1 g fiber, 19 g pro.*

easy minestrone

Start to Finish: 25 minutes   Makes 4 servings (1¾ cups each)

1   28-ounce can diced tomatoes with Italian herbs, undrained
2   cups water
1   14- to 15-ounce can garbanzo beans (chickpeas), rinsed and drained
1   cup low-sodium vegetable broth or reduced-sodium chicken broth
¾   cup chopped yellow sweet pepper or ½ cup thinly sliced carrot
2   teaspoons dried Italian seasoning, crushed, or 1 teaspoon garlic powder plus
    1 teaspoon dried basil, crushed
1   cup dried rigatoni or penne pasta
2   to 3 cups fresh baby spinach
    Shaved Parmesan cheese and/or fresh basil (optional)

1. In a 4-quart Dutch oven combine the first six ingredients (through Italian seasoning). Stir in pasta. Bring to boiling; reduce heat. Cook, covered, about 10 minutes or just until pasta is barely tender, stirring occasionally. Stir in spinach. If desired, top with Parmesan cheese and/or basil.

Per Serving: *234 cal., 2 g fat (0 g sat. fat), 0 mg chol., 759 mg sodium, 46 g carb., 12 g sugars, 7 g fiber, 10 g pro.*

PERFECT PAIR   Add a salad of fresh baby romaine, crushed whole grain croutons, some toasted pine nuts, sliced cremini mushrooms, and slivered red onion dressed with a balsamic vinaigrette.

fresh taco salad

Start to Finish: 30 minutes   Makes 6 servings (2¼ cups each)

- 4   cups mixed salad greens
- 1   15-ounce can black beans, rinsed and drained
- 2   ears fresh sweet corn, husks and silks removed and kernels cut off the cobs
- ¾   cup matchstick-size pieces peeled jicama
- ½   cup chopped tomato
- 1   medium avocado, halved, seeded, peeled, and sliced
- 1   fresh jalapeño chile pepper, stemmed, seeded, and thinly sliced*
- 2   cups multigrain tortilla chips with flaxseeds
- ½   cup refrigerated fresh salsa
- ½   cup crumbled queso fresco (2 ounces)
- 1   recipe Cilantro Ranch Dressing

SIMPLE SWAP

If fresh corn isn't in season, use 1 cup frozen whole kernel corn, thawed.

1. Line a large platter with salad greens. In a medium bowl combine the next four ingredients (through tomato). Spoon over greens. Arrange avocado and chile pepper slices over top. Top with chips, salsa, and cheese. Drizzle with Cilantro Ranch Dressing.

CILANTRO RANCH DRESSING: In a bowl whisk together ⅓ cup light sour cream; ¼ cup buttermilk; 2 tablespoons snipped fresh cilantro; 1 tablespoon snipped fresh chives; 1 tablespoon lime juice; 2 cloves garlic, minced; and 1 teaspoon chili powder.

*TIP: Chile peppers contain oils that can irritate your skin and eyes. Wear plastic or rubber gloves when working with them.

Per Serving: *214 cal., 9 g fat (3 g sat. fat), 11 mg chol., 447 mg sodium, 29 g carb., 4 g sugars, 8 g fiber, 10 g pro.*

muenster, cabbage, and apple sandwiches

Start to Finish: 30 minutes   Makes 4 servings (1 sandwich each)

- 1 medium onion, halved lengthwise and thinly sliced
- ¼ cup cider vinegar
- ¼ cup water
- 1 cup coarsely shredded cabbage
- 1 large cooking apple, such as Granny Smith, Rome Beauty, or Jonathan, thinly sliced
- 1 tablespoon stone-ground mustard
- 1 cup shredded Muenster cheese (4 ounces)
- 8 slices caraway rye bread
  Nonstick cooking spray

SIMPLE SWAP

Change it up with a pear instead of an apple or cheddar cheese for Muenster.

1. In a medium skillet combine onion, vinegar, and the water. Bring just to boiling; reduce heat. Simmer, covered, 3 minutes. Stir in cabbage; simmer, covered, 3 minutes. Stir in apple slices. Simmer, covered, about 3 minutes more or just until vegetables and apple are tender; drain. Stir in mustard.

2. Layer cabbage mixture and the cheese on four bread slices. Top with the remaining bread slices. Lightly coat outsides of sandwiches with cooking spray.

3. Preheat a large nonstick skillet over medium heat. Place sandwiches, half at a time if necessary, in skillet. Weight down with a heavy skillet and cook 1 to 2 minutes or until bread is toasted. Turn sandwiches, weight down again, and cook 1 to 2 minutes more or until bread is toasted and filling is heated.

Per Serving: *296 cal., 11 g fat (6 g sat. fat), 27 mg chol., 606 mg sodium, 39 g carb., 10 g sugars, 5 g fiber, 12 g pro.*

cauliflower-crusted pizza

Prep: 30 minutes   Microwave: 3 minutes   Bake: 17 minutes at 425°F   Makes 4 servings (2 slices each)

4   cups cauliflower florets
1   egg, lightly beaten
¼   cup shredded Italian cheese blend
¼   cup grated Parmesan cheese
¼   cup panko bread crumbs
½   teaspoon dried Italian seasoning, crushed
¼   teaspoon salt
2   cups sliced fresh mushrooms
1   cup yellow or green sweet pepper strips
1   small red onion, cut into thin wedges
1   teaspoon olive oil
¾   cup Quick Pizza Sauce
1   cup shredded Italian cheese blend (4 ounces)
    Snipped fresh basil, oregano, and/or parsley (optional)

SIMPLE SWAP

Use canned pizza or pasta sauce for the Quick Pizza Sauce.

1. Place the cauliflower in a food processor. Cover and pulse four to six times or until crumbly and mixture resembles the texture of couscous.

2. Place a pizza stone or baking sheet in the oven. Preheat oven to 425°F. Place cauliflower in a microwave-safe casserole with 2 tablespoons water. Microwave, covered, 3 to 4 minutes or until tender, stirring once or twice. Cool. Transfer cauliflower to a 100-percent-cotton flour sack towel. Wrap towel around cauliflower and squeeze until there is no more liquid (this step is critical).

3. For crust, in a bowl stir together drained cauliflower and the next six ingredients (through salt). On a piece of parchment paper, pat cauliflower mixture into a 12-inch circle. Transfer crust on paper to the preheated pizza stone. Bake 12 to 15 minutes or until crisp and starting to brown.

4. Meanwhile, in a large skillet cook and stir the next three ingredients (through onion) in hot oil 4 to 6 minutes or until crisp-tender. Remove from heat.

5. Spread pizza sauce over baked crust. Top with cooked vegetables. Sprinkle with the 1 cup Italian cheese blend. Bake about 5 minutes more or until heated and cheese melts. If desired, sprinkle with snipped fresh herbs. Cut into slices.

QUICK PIZZA SAUCE: In a small saucepan cook ½ cup chopped onion and 2 cloves garlic, minced, in 1 tablespoon hot oil over medium heat about 5 minutes or until tender, stirring occasionally. Stir in one 8-ounce can tomato sauce; ½ teaspoon each dried oregano and basil, crushed; and ¼ teaspoon each salt and crushed red pepper. Bring to boiling; reduce heat. Simmer, uncovered, about 5 minutes or until sauce reaches desired consistency.

Per Serving: *264 cal., 14 g fat (7 g sat. fat), 76 mg chol., 893 mg sodium, 18 g carb., 7 g sugars, 4 g fiber, 17 g pro.*

roasted vegetable flatbread

Prep: 20 minutes   Roast: 15 minutes at 475°F   Makes 4 servings (1 flatbread each)

3 cups sliced fresh mushrooms
2 cups cut-up asparagus, green beans, zucchini, and/or sugar snap pea pods
2 medium yellow sweet peppers, seeded and cut into thin bite-size strips
2 medium red onions, sliced
4 teaspoons olive oil
¼ teaspoon salt
4 whole wheat flatbreads
⅓ cup grated Pecorino Romano cheese
2 cups halved cherry tomatoes
½ cup shredded part-skim mozzarella cheese (2 ounces)

1. Preheat oven to 475°F. Line a large baking sheet with parchment paper; set aside. In a large bowl combine the first six ingredients (through salt). Spoon vegetable mixture evenly onto the prepared baking sheet. Roast 10 minutes; remove from oven.

2. Place flatbreads on two large baking sheets; sprinkle with Pecorino Romano cheese. Top with roasted vegetables and cherry tomatoes; sprinkle with mozzarella cheese. Roast about 5 minutes more or until mozzarella cheese is melted.

Per Serving: 300 cal., 12 g fat (3 g sat. fat), 16 mg chol., 635 mg sodium, 41 g carb., 11 g sugars, 10 g fiber, 17 g pro.

PERFECT PAIR   Top a wedge of crisp iceberg lettuce or baby romaine with a drizzle of light creamy dressing of your choice and a sprinkling of chopped red onion and halved grape tomatoes.

tofu stir-fry with soba noodles

Start to Finish: 25 minutes   Makes 4 servings (1 cup each)

 5 ounces dried soba (buckwheat noodles)
 2 teaspoons toasted sesame oil
 2 cloves garlic, minced
 1 teaspoon grated fresh ginger
 1¼ cups coarsely chopped red sweet pepper
 12 ounces firm tub-style tofu (fresh bean curd), drained and cubed
 3 tablespoons snipped fresh cilantro or basil (optional)
 3 tablespoons reduced-sodium teriyaki sauce
 1 tablespoon water
 4 cups packaged fresh baby spinach

SIMPLE SWAP

Sliced bok choy is a crunchy substitute for spinach.

1. Cook soba according to package directions; drain. Return to hot pan; cover and keep warm.

2. Meanwhile, in a large skillet heat sesame oil over medium-high heat. Add garlic and ginger; cook and stir 30 seconds. Add sweet pepper; cook and stir 2 minutes. Add tofu; cook 1 minute more, stirring gently.

3. Stir in cilantro (if desired), teriyaki sauce, and the water. Gradually add spinach, stirring just until spinach is wilted. Serve with cooked soba.

Per Serving: *300 cal., 10 g fat (1 g sat. fat), 0 mg chol., 648 mg sodium, 37 g carb., 4 sugars, 5 g fiber, 37 g pro.*

up to
400 calories

AS YOU FIND SUCCESS WITH WEIGHT LOSS, YOU
CAN INCREASE THE NUMBER OF CALORIES OVER THE
COURSE OF THE DAY. LOOK HERE FOR HEALTHFUL
RECIPES THAT BUMP UP THE ENERGY COUNT.

cheesy potato bake with eggs

Prep: 35 minutes   Bake: 1 hour 40 minutes at 325°F   Makes 8 servings (about 1 cup each)

- 2 **tablespoons butter**
- ½ **cup finely chopped onion**
- 4 **teaspoons all-purpose flour**
- 1 **teaspoon salt**
- ½ **teaspoon black pepper**
- 1½ **cups fat-free milk**
- 2 **cups reduced-fat shredded sharp cheddar cheese (8 ounces)**
- 3 pounds russet potatoes, peeled and sliced ⅛ inch thick*
- 1 **tablespoon vegetable oil**
- 1½ **cups chopped fresh or frozen broccoli**
- 8 **eggs**
- 2 **tablespoons water**
- 6 **slices lower-sodium, less-fat bacon, crisp-cooked, drained, and crumbled**
- ¾ **cup chopped tomato**

SIMPLE SWAP

For even faster preparation, purchase sliced fresh potatoes, such as Simply Potatoes brand.

1. Preheat oven to 325°F. For cheese sauce, in a medium saucepan melt butter over medium heat. Add onion; cook about 4 minutes or until tender, stirring occasionally. Stir in flour, ½ teaspoon of the salt, and ¼ teaspoon of the pepper. Stir in milk; cook and stir until slightly thickened and bubbly. Add cheese; stir just until melted. Remove from heat.

2. In a 3-quart rectangular baking dish spread half the potatoes in an even layer. Spread half the cheese sauce over the potatoes. Repeat with the remaining potatoes and cheese sauce. Bake, covered, 1 hour 30 minutes or until potatoes are tender. Uncover and bake 10 minutes more.

3. In a large skillet heat oil over medium heat. Add broccoli; cook about 5 minutes or until nearly tender, stirring frequently. In a bowl beat together eggs, the water, the remaining ½ teaspoon salt, and the remaining ¼ teaspoon pepper. Pour over broccoli in skillet. Cook, without stirring, until mixture begins to set on the bottom and around the edges. Using a spatula, lift and fold the partially cooked egg mixture so the uncooked portion flows underneath. Continue cooking about 2 minutes more or until egg mixture is cooked but is still glossy and moist. Spoon eggs over potatoes. Top with bacon and chopped tomato. Serve immediately.

*TIP: To slice potatoes quickly, use a food processor fitted with a slicing blade or use a mandoline slicer.

Per Serving: *341 cal., 17 g fat (8 g sat. fat), 217 mg chol., 701 mg sodium, 30 g carb., 5 g sugars, 3 g fiber, 20 g pro.*

pan-roasted vegetable quinoa with eggs

Start to Finish: 40 minutes   Makes 4 servings (1¼ cups quinoa mixture and 1 egg each)

- 2   cups reduced-sodium vegetable broth or water
- 1   cup quinoa, rinsed and drained
- 2   cups sliced cremini mushrooms
- 1   large red onion, cut into thin wedges
- 1   cup sliced halved yellow summer squash
- 1   tablespoon olive oil
- 2   cups torn fresh baby kale or spinach
- 1   cup grape tomatoes, halved
- 1   teaspoon fresh thyme leaves
- ¼   teaspoon salt
- ¼   teaspoon black pepper
- 2   teaspoons olive oil
- 4   eggs

SIMPLE SWAP

Use desired seasonal vegetables, such as sweet peppers, asparagus, and/or snow peas.

1. In a medium saucepan bring broth to boiling; stir in quinoa. Reduce heat. Simmer, covered, about 15 minutes or until quinoa is tender. Drain if necessary.

2. Meanwhile, in a large skillet cook mushrooms, onion, and yellow squash in the 1 tablespoon hot oil over medium-high heat about 5 minutes or until tender and lightly browned, stirring frequently. Stir in the next five ingredients (through pepper). Reduce heat to medium. Cook about 3 minutes or until tomatoes soften. Stir vegetables into cooked quinoa.

3. Wipe out skillet. Heat the 2 teaspoons oil in the same skillet over medium heat. Break eggs into skillet. Reduce heat to low. Cook eggs 3 to 4 minutes or until whites are completely set and yolks start to thicken. If desired, turn the eggs and cook 30 seconds more (for over-easy). Serve eggs over quinoa mixture. If desired, sprinkle eggs with additional pepper.

Per Serving: *342 cal., 14 g fat (3 g sat. fat), 186 mg chol., 515 mg sodium, 39 g carb., 6 g sugars, 6 g fiber, 18 g pro.*

chicken breakfast burritos

Start to Finish: 45 minutes   Makes 8 servings (1 burrito each)

- 3 tablespoons butter
- 1½ cups refrigerated shredded hash brown potatoes
- 2 cloves garlic, minced
- ¼ teaspoon ground cumin
- ¾ cup chopped cooked chicken breast
- 6 eggs
- ⅓ cup milk
- ¼ teaspoon salt
- ⅛ teaspoon black pepper
- 8 10-inch flour tortillas, warmed*
- 1 4-ounce can diced green chile peppers, drained
- ½ cup bottled salsa
- 1 cup shredded reduced-fat Colby and Monterey Jack cheese (4 ounces)

SIMPLE SWAP

For verde burritos, use green chile salsa.

1. In a large nonstick skillet melt 2 tablespoons of the butter over medium heat. Stir in potatoes, garlic, and cumin. Spread in an even layer, pressing down lightly with a spatula. Cook 6 to 7 minutes or until golden brown on the bottom. Turn potatoes over; spread evenly and press down lightly. Cook 6 to 8 minutes more or until golden brown and crisp. Stir in chicken. Remove from skillet.

2. In a medium bowl whisk together the next four ingredients (through black pepper). In the same skillet melt the remaining 1 tablespoon butter over medium heat. Add egg mixture. Cook over medium heat, without stirring, until mixture begins to set on bottom and around edges. Lift and fold the partially cooked egg mixture so the uncooked portion flows underneath. Continue cooking 2 to 3 minutes or until egg mixture is cooked through but is still glossy and moist. Remove from heat.

3. Spoon potato mixture just below the centers of warm tortillas. Top with egg mixture, chile peppers, salsa, and cheese. Fold bottom edge of each tortilla up and over filling. Fold in the opposite sides and roll up.

*TIP: To warm tortillas, stack tortillas and wrap in microwave-safe paper towels. Microwave about 1 minute or until heated.

Per Serving: *398 cal., 16 g fat (7 g sat. fat), 173 mg chol., 739 mg sodium, 40 g carb., 1 g sugars, 2 g fiber, 20 g pro.*

turkey sausage breakfast sandwiches

Start to Finish: 25 minutes   Makes 4 servings (1 sandwich each)

- ¼ **cup light mayonnaise**
- 2 **teaspoons sriracha sauce**
- 8 **ounces bulk lean ground turkey sausage**
- ¼ **cup finely chopped red sweet pepper**
- 2 **tablespoons finely chopped green onion**
  Nonstick cooking spray
- 4 **eggs**
- ¼ **cup shredded white cheddar cheese or sharp cheddar cheese (1 ounce)**
- 4 multigrain sandwich thins, toasted if desired
- 2 **cups fresh baby spinach or arugula**

SIMPLE SWAP

Use whole grain English muffins for the sandwich thins.

1. In a bowl stir together mayonnaise and sriracha sauce. In another bowl combine sausage, sweet pepper, and onion. Using wet hands, form mixture into four 4-inch patties. Coat an extra-large nonstick skillet with cooking spray; heat over medium heat. Add patties; cook about 2 minutes per side or until browned and no longer pink in the center.

2. Meanwhile, coat a large skillet with cooking spray; heat over medium heat. Break eggs into skillet. Reduce heat to medium-low; cook eggs 3 to 4 minutes or until whites are completely set and yolks start to thicken. Turn eggs over; break yolks slightly with the spatula. Sprinkle with cheese. Cook 1 to 2 minutes more or until yolks are just set.

3. Spread sandwich thins with mayonnaise mixture and fill with spinach, sausage patties, and eggs.

Per Serving: 339 cal., 16 g fat (5 g sat. fat), 238 mg chol., 860 mg sodium, 26 g carb., 4 g sugars, 6 g fiber, 24 g pro.

multigrain citrus waffles

Prep: 15 minutes   Bake: according to waffle baker manufacturer's instructions
Makes 6 servings (2 [4-inch] waffles each)

1½   cups all-purpose flour
½   cup whole wheat flour
½   cup oat flour
1   tablespoon baking powder
1   tablespoon packed brown sugar
½   teaspoon baking soda
¼   teaspoon salt
2   eggs, lightly beaten
1¾   cups fat-free milk or low-fat vanilla soymilk
⅓   cup canola oil
1   tablespoon orange zest
¾   cup low-sugar orange marmalade, warmed

1. In a bowl stir together the first seven ingredients (through salt). Make a well in the center of flour mixture. In another bowl combine the next four ingredients (through orange zest). Add egg mixture all at once to flour mixture. Stir just until moistened (batter should be slightly lumpy).

2. Using a regular or Belgian waffle maker, bake waffles according to the manufacturer's directions. Close lid quickly; do not open until done. Serve waffles warm with marmalade.

Per Serving: *394 cal., 15 g fat (2 g sat. fat), 63 mg chol., 501 mg sodium, 55 g carb., 16 g sugars, 3 g fiber, 10 g pro.*

PERFECT PAIR   Serve these waffles with individual bowls of fresh berries topped with plain fat-free yogurt sweetened with a touch of maple syrup or honey.

cheddar-bacon waffles

Prep: 25 minutes   Stand: 1 hour   Bake: according to waffle baker manufacturer's instructions
Makes 8 servings (1 waffle each)

- 1¾ cups all-purpose flour
- ½ cup whole wheat flour
- 1¾ cups warm low-fat milk (105°F to 115°F)
- 1 tablespoon sugar
- 1 package active dry yeast
- 2 eggs, lightly beaten
- ⅓ cup butter, melted
- 1 2.8-ounce package real bacon pieces
- 1 cup finely shredded reduced-fat mild cheddar cheese (4 ounces)
- Pure maple syrup

1. Place flours in a bowl; make a well in the center.

2. In another bowl combine ½ cup of the milk, the sugar, and yeast. Let stand 10 minutes or until foamy. In a third bowl combine the remaining 1¼ cups milk, the eggs, and melted butter.

3. Add egg mixture and yeast mixture to the flours. Stir just until moistened (batter should still be slightly lumpy). Cover with plastic wrap and let stand at room temperature 1 hour. Gently fold in bacon pieces and cheese.

4. Add batter to a preheated, well-greased Belgian waffle maker and bake according to manufacturer's directions, using about ⅔ cup batter per waffle. When done, use a fork to lift waffle off grid. Repeat with remaining batter.* Serve warm with maple syrup.

*TIP: Keep finished waffles warm by placing them in a single layer on a baking sheet. Hold in a 200°F oven until all waffles are baked.

Per Serving: 369 cal., 15 g fat (8 g sat. fat), 87 mg chol., 504 mg sodium, 45 g carb., 16 g sugars, 2 g fiber, 15 g pro.

PERFECT PAIR   Serve these hearty waffles with a fruit salad of ruby red grapefruit and orange sections sprinkled with pomegranate seeds. If desired, drizzle salad with a little pure maple syrup or honey.

berry breakfast pizzas

Start to Finish: 25 minutes   Makes 4 servings (1 pizza each)

¼   cup granulated sugar
4   teaspoons cornstarch
     Dash salt
½   cup water
2   cups mixed fresh berries, such as blueberries, raspberries, and/or blackberries
1   teaspoon butter
1   teaspoon orange zest
4   ounces reduced-fat cream cheese (Neufchâtel), softened
2   tablespoons orange marmalade
2   teaspoons granulated sugar
¼   teaspoon ground cardamom
2   pita bread rounds, split
2   tablespoons butter, melted
     Powdered sugar (optional)

SIMPLE SWAP

If you don't have cardamom, substitute ground cinnamon or apple pie spice.

1. For berry topping, in a medium saucepan combine the first three ingredients (through salt). Stir in the water. Stir in ½ cup of the berries. Cook and stir over medium heat until thickened. Remove from heat. Add 1 cup of the remaining berries and the 1 teaspoon butter, stirring until butter is melted. Gently stir in orange zest.

2. In a bowl beat cream cheese and orange marmalade with a mixer on low to medium until smooth. In another bowl stir together the 2 teaspoons granulated sugar and the cardamom.

3. Toast the split pita rounds. Brush pita rounds with the 2 tablespoons melted butter; sprinkle with the sugar-cardamom mixture. Spread cream cheese mixture on pita rounds; top with berry topping. Top with the remaining ½ cup berries. If desired, sprinkle with powdered sugar.

TO MAKE AHEAD: Make the berry topping as directed in Step 1; cool completely. Cover and chill up to 8 hours.

Per Serving: *343 cal., 14 g fat (8 g sat. fat), 39 mg chol., 359 mg sodium, 51 g carb., 27 g sugars, 4 g fiber, 6 g pro.*

355 CALORIES ☐ GLUTEN-FREE ☑ MAKE-AHEAD ☑ HIGH-FIBER ☐ 30-MINUTE ☑ VEGETARIAN

peanut butter-banana overnight oatmeal

Prep: 10 minutes   Chill: overnight   Makes 2 servings (about 1 cup each)

1   6-ounce carton plain low-fat yogurt or
    one 5.3-ounce carton plain whole-milk
    Greek yogurt
⅔   cup regular rolled oats
⅔   cup milk
½   cup sliced banana

2   tablespoons honey
1   tablespoon chia seeds or flaxseed meal
    (optional)
1   tablespoon peanut butter
    Banana slices, fresh blueberries,
    and/or honey (optional)

1. In a bowl stir together the first seven ingredients (through peanut butter). If desired, transfer mixture into a pint jar with a lid or two half-pint jars with lids. Cover; chill overnight or up to 3 days.

2. To serve, spoon oatmeal into a cereal bowl(s). If desired, top with additional banana slices, blueberries, and/or a drizzle of honey.

Per Serving: 355 cal., 9 g fat (3 g sat. fat), 12 mg chol., 136 mg sodium, 60 g carb., 36 g sugars, 5 g fiber, 13 g pro.

PERFECT PAIR   This satisfying breakfast is great when you are on the go. Add some additional fresh fruit or fruit juice for a complete meal.

352 CALORIES ☐ GLUTEN-FREE ☑ MAKE-AHEAD ☐ HIGH-FIBER ☐ 30-MINUTE ☐ VEGETARIAN

carrot cake overnight oatmeal

Prep: 10 minutes   Chill: overnight   Makes 2 servings (about 1 cup each)

1   6-ounce carton plain low-fat yogurt or
    one 5.3-ounce carton plain whole-milk
    Greek yogurt
⅔   cup regular rolled oats
⅔   cup milk
⅓   cup finely shredded carrot
2   tablespoons raisins
2   tablespoons crushed pineapple

2   tablespoons pure maple syrup
1   tablespoon chia seeds or flaxseed meal
    (optional)
¼   teaspoon ground cinnamon
2   tablespoons chopped walnuts, toasted
    Crushed pineapple (optional)
    Toasted flaked coconut (optional)

SIMPLE SWAP

Dried cranberries
are a tangy trade
for raisins.

1. In a bowl combine the first nine ingredients (through cinnamon). If desired, transfer mixture to a pint jar with a lid or two half-pint jars with lids. Cover and chill overnight or up to 3 days.

2. To serve, spoon oatmeal into a cereal bowl(s). Top with walnuts and, if desired, additional pineapple and toasted coconut.

Per Serving: 352 cal., 10 g fat (3 g sat. fat), 12 mg chol., 116 mg sodium, 57 g carb., 36 g sugars, 4 g fiber, 12 g pro.

farro cereal with pears, walnuts, and cherries

Prep: 10 minutes   Cook: 35 minutes   Makes 4 servings (¾ cup farro and about ¼ cup pear mixture each)

- 3 **cups water**
- 1 **cup pearled or semipearled farro**
- ¼ **teaspoon salt**
- 1 **tablespoon butter**
- 1 medium ripe pear, cored and cut up
- ½ **cup chopped toasted walnuts**
- ⅓ **cup dried tart cherries**
- ¼ **teaspoon ground cinnamon**
- ¼ **cup fat-free half-and-half**
- 2 **tablespoons maple syrup**

SIMPLE SWAP

Apples, pecans, and raisins turn this into an apple crisp-tasting breakfast.

1. In a medium saucepan combine the water, farro, and salt. Bring to boiling; reduce heat. Simmer, covered, 25 to 30 minutes or until farro is tender. Drain if necessary.

2. Meanwhile, in a medium skillet cook pear in hot butter over medium heat until tender. Stir in nuts, cherries, and cinnamon. Spoon over hot farro. Drizzle with half-and-half and maple syrup.

Per Serving: *394 cal., 14 g fat (3 g sat. fat), 8 mg chol., 192 mg sodium, 62 g carb., 20 g sugars, 8 g fiber, 10 g pro.*

soy-glazed flank steak with blistered green beans

Prep: 20 minutes   Cook: 15 minutes   Makes 4 servings (1½ cups each)

- 1 **pound green beans**
- 1 **pound beef flank steak**
- 6 **cloves garlic, minced (1 tablespoon)**
- 1 **tablespoon finely chopped fresh ginger**
- 2 **tablespoons soy sauce**
- 1 **teaspoon packed brown sugar**
- 2 **to 3 tablespoons peanut oil**
- 4 **green onions, white parts only, thinly sliced**
- 2 **tablespoons sweet rice wine (mirin)**
- 1 **teaspoon red chile paste (sambal oelek)**
  Hot cooked jasmine rice (optional)
  Sesame seeds, toasted (optional)

SIMPLE SWAP

If you don't have red chile paste, sriracha sauce adds heat, too.

1. Trim and halve green beans on the diagonal. Cut flank steak across the grain into thin slices. In a bowl combine garlic and ginger. In another bowl combine soy sauce and brown sugar.

2. In an extra-large skillet or wok heat 2 tablespoons oil over medium-high heat. Add green beans; cook and stir 7 to 8 minutes or until beans are blistered and brown in spots. Transfer beans to paper towels to drain. If necessary, add the remaining 1 tablespoon oil to skillet.

3. Add garlic-ginger mixture to skillet; cook and stir 30 seconds. Add half of the beef strips to skillet. Cook and stir about 3 minutes or until beef is browned. Using a slotted spoon, transfer mixture to a bowl. Repeat with the remaining beef. Return all beef to skillet. Stir in green onions, rice wine, chile paste, and the soy sauce-sugar mixture; cook and stir 1 minute. Add green beans; cook and stir about 2 minutes or until beans are heated. If desired, serve with hot cooked rice and sprinkle with sesame seeds.

Per Serving: 312 cal., 16 g fat (5 g sat. fat), 53 mg chol., 672 mg sodium, 15 g carb., 8 g sugars, 4 g fiber, 28 g pro.

grilled flank steak salad

Prep: 30 minutes   Marinate: 30 minutes   Grill: 17 minutes

Makes 4 servings (3 ounces steak, 1 cup greens, ½ cup vegetables, and 1½ tablespoons dressing each)

- 1   **recipe Cilantro Dressing**
- 1   **pound beef flank steak**
- 4   **small yellow and/or red sweet peppers, halved**
- 2   **ears fresh sweet corn**
- 4   **green onions, trimmed**
     Nonstick cooking spray
- 4   **cups torn romaine lettuce**
- 8   **cherry tomatoes, halved**
- ½   **of a small avocado, peeled and thinly sliced (optional)**

1. Prepare Cilantro Dressing and divide it into two portions.

2. Score both sides of steak in a diamond pattern by making shallow diagonal cuts at 1-inch intervals. Place steak in a resealable plastic bag set in a shallow dish. Pour one portion of the Cilantro Dressing over steak. Seal bag; turn to coat steak. Marinate in the refrigerator 30 minutes.

3. Coat sweet peppers, corn, and green onions with cooking spray. Grill steak and corn, uncovered, over medium heat until steak is desired doneness and corn is tender, turning steak once and turning corn occasionally. For steak, allow 17 to 21 minutes for medium rare (145°F) to medium (160°F). For corn, allow 15 to 20 minutes. Add sweet pepper halves the last 8 minutes of grilling and green onions to the grill the last 4 minutes of grilling, turning frequently.

4. Thinly slice steak against the grain. Coarsely chop sweet peppers and green onions; cut corn from cob, leaving kernels in "sheets." Top romaine lettuce with steak, grilled vegetables, tomatoes, and, if desired, avocado slices. Drizzle with the reserved portion of Cilantro Dressing.

CILANTRO DRESSING: In a blender or food processor combine ⅓ cup lime juice; ¼ cup each chopped shallots and snipped fresh cilantro; 2 tablespoons each olive oil and water; 4 teaspoons honey; 2 cloves garlic, peeled and quartered; 1 teaspoon chili powder; and ½ teaspoon each salt and ground cumin. Cover and blend until combined.

Per Serving: *337 cal., 12 g fat (3 g sat. fat), 47 mg chol., 375 mg sodium, 31 g carb., 13 g sugars, 5 g fiber, 29 g pro.*

PERFECT PAIR   For a quick accompaniment to this salad, rub thick slices of multigrain Italian bread with crushed garlic and brush with olive oil before toasting on the grill.

beef stew pot pie

Prep: 25 minutes   Bake: 20 minutes at 375°F   Makes 8 servings (1 cup each)

Nonstick cooking spray

¼ cup butter

3 croissants, split

1½ cups coarsely chopped carrots

1½ cups coarsely chopped celery

1 cup frozen small whole onions, thawed and halved

3 cups sliced fresh mushrooms

1 cup red wine, such as Burgundy

1 tablespoon stone-ground Dijon-style mustard

4 cloves garlic, minced

2 teaspoons snipped fresh rosemary

2 teaspoons dried thyme, crushed

½ teaspoon black pepper

2 17-ounce packages refrigerated cooked beef tips with gravy

1 cup 50%-less-sodium beef broth

1. Preheat oven to 375°F. Coat a 3-quart rectangular baking dish with cooking spray.

2. In a bowl microwave 1 tablespoon of the butter on 70% power (medium-high) about 30 seconds or until melted. Brush cut sides of croissants with melted butter. Cube croissants; set aside.

3. In a large skillet melt the remaining 3 tablespoons butter over medium heat. Add carrots, celery, and onions. Cook 7 to 9 minutes or just until vegetables are tender, stirring occasionally. Carefully stir in the next seven ingredients (through pepper). Bring to boiling; reduce heat. Simmer, uncovered, 5 minutes. Stir in beef with gravy and the broth; heat.

4. Transfer hot meat mixture to the prepared baking dish. Sprinkle with cubed croissants. Bake, uncovered, 20 to 25 minutes or until bubbly and croissants are golden.

Per Serving: 330 cal., 16 g fat (8 g sat. fat), 77 mg chol., 885 mg sodium, 21 g carb., 8 g sugars, 3 g fiber, 21 g pro.

PERFECT PAIR   Balance this rich-tasting casserole with a zippy slaw of shaved Brussels sprouts, thinly sliced red onion, quartered grape tomatoes, snipped fresh parsley, and a red wine vinaigrette.

pasta with garlicky steak and red onions

Start to Finish: 30 minutes   Makes 6 servings (1¾ cups each)

SIMPLE SWAP

Any short pasta shape works well in this dish. Choose your favorite multigrain brand for the biggest nutritional bang.

1	14.5 ounce box dried multigrain penne pasta
12	ounces boneless beef sirloin steak
2	tablespoons olive oil
1	medium red onion, quartered and thinly sliced
1	medium red sweet pepper, cut into strips (optional)
4	cloves garlic, minced
¾	teaspoon salt
¼	teaspoon crushed red pepper
1	cup reduced-sodium chicken broth
4	cups fresh baby spinach
1	tablespoon snipped fresh basil or thyme
¼	cup shaved Parmesan cheese (1 ounce) (optional)

1. Cook pasta in lightly salted water according to package directions. Drain, reserving ¼ cup of the pasta cooking water. Return pasta to hot pan; cover and keep warm.

2. Meanwhile, trim fat from meat. Thinly slice meat across the grain into bite-size strips. In an extra-large nonstick skillet heat 1 tablespoon of the oil over medium-high heat. Add meat; cook and stir 3 to 4 minutes or until meat is slightly pink in center. Remove from skillet; keep warm.

3. Add the next five ingredients (through crushed red pepper) to skillet. Cook about 8 minutes or until onion is tender, stirring occasionally. Add broth and the reserved pasta cooking water; bring to boiling. Add the remaining 1 tablespoon oil, the meat, onion mixture, spinach, and basil to cooked pasta; toss just until spinach is wilted. Top with Parmesan cheese and/or additional crushed red pepper.

Per Serving: *392 cal., 9 g fat (1 g sat. fat), 39 mg chol., 481 mg sodium, 51 g carb., 4 g sugars, 6 g fiber, 27 g pro.*

kansas city steak soup

Prep: 20 minutes   Cook: 20 minutes   Heat: 30 minutes   Makes 6 servings (2 cups each)

1½ **pounds lean ground beef**
1 **cup chopped onion**
1 **cup sliced celery**
2 **14.5-ounce cans 50%-less-sodium beef broth**
1 **28-ounce can diced tomatoes, undrained**
1 **10-ounce package frozen mixed vegetables**
2 **tablespoons steak sauce**
2 **teaspoons Worcestershire sauce**
¼ **teaspoon salt**
¼ **teaspoon black pepper**
¼ **cup all-purpose flour**
   Snipped fresh Italian parsley

1. In a large Dutch oven cook ground beef, onion, and celery over medium-high heat until meat is browned and vegetables are tender. Drain off fat.

2. Stir in one can of the broth and the next six ingredients (through pepper). Bring to boiling; reduce heat. Simmer, covered, 20 minutes.

3. In a bowl whisk together the remaining can of broth and the flour; stir into Dutch oven. Cook over medium-high heat until thickened and bubbly, stirring occasionally. Cook and stir 1 minute more. Sprinkle soup with parsley.

TO MAKE AHEAD: Cool soup slightly. Transfer to an airtight container. Cover and chill for up to 3 days. To serve, heat soup in a large Dutch oven over medium heat about 30 minutes or until heated through, stirring occasionally.

Per Serving: *306 cal., 12 g fat (5 g sat. fat), 74 mg chol., 747 mg sodium, 21 g carb., 8 g sugars, 4 g fiber, 27 g pro.*

PERFECT PAIR   Keep up the steakhouse vibe. Serve this soup with a classic iceberg lettuce wedge salad topped with a drizzle of reduced-fat blue cheese dressing and crumbled crisp-cooked lower-sodium, less-fat bacon.

cheeseburger galettes

Prep: 40 minutes   Bake: 15 minutes at 400°F   Makes 6 servings (1 galette each)

Nonstick cooking spray
1 pound 90% lean ground beef
¾ cup chopped green or red sweet pepper
2 cloves garlic, minced
1 8-ounce can no-salt-added tomato sauce
⅓ cup sliced dill pickles, chopped
2 tablespoons yellow mustard
1 13.8-ounce package refrigerated pizza dough with whole grain
¾ cup shredded reduced-fat cheddar cheese (3 ounces)
¼ cup chopped red onion

1. Preheat oven to 400°F. Line a large baking sheet with foil; spray with cooking spray. In a large skillet cook beef, sweet pepper, and garlic over medium heat until meat is browned; drain off fat. Stir in tomato sauce, chopped pickles, and mustard.

2. Unroll the pizza crust on a lightly floured surface. Cut into six equal portions. Roll and stretch portions to 6-inch squares. Place squares on the prepared baking sheet. Spoon beef mixture onto centers of dough squares, leaving a 1-inch border. Top with cheese. Fold dough up over edges of filling, pleating and pinching as necessary.

3. Bake about 15 minutes or until crust is golden. Top galettes with onion and, if desired, additional sliced dill pickles.

Per Serving: 381 cal., 15 g fat (5 g sat. fat), 58 mg chol., 672 mg sodium, 36 g carb., 6 g sugars, 4 g fiber, 24 g pro.

PERFECT PAIR   For a nutrition boost, serve galettes with a traditional creamy broccoli salad. Toss broccoli florets with chopped onion, raisins, crumbled crisp-cooked bacon, and a dressing of light mayonnaise with a spoonful of sugar and a splash of cider vinegar.

barley tabbouleh with lebanese meatballs

Prep: 30 minutes   Cook: 40 minutes   Makes 6 servings (2 meatballs and 1⅓ cups tabbouleh each)

3½ cups reduced-sodium chicken broth or water
 1 cup hull-less barley* or regular pearled barley
 2 cups snipped fresh parsley
 2 cups chopped unpeeled seedless cucumber
 1 15-ounce can garbanzo beans (chickpeas), rinsed and drained
 1 cup chopped tomatoes
 ½ cup finely chopped red onion
 2 cloves garlic, minced
 ¼ cup lemon juice
1½ tablespoons olive oil
 ¼ teaspoon salt
 ¼ teaspoon black pepper
 1 recipe Lebanese Meatballs
 ¾ cup plain fat-free Greek yogurt (optional)

SIMPLE SWAP

For more authenticity, use ground lamb for all or part of the ground beef.

1. For tabbouleh, in a large saucepan combine broth and barley. Bring to boiling; reduce heat. Simmer, uncovered, 30 to 40 minutes or until desired tenderness; drain. Transfer barley to a bowl and let cool. Stir in the next five ingredients (through onion). In another bowl whisk together the next five ingredients (through pepper). Add to barley mixture; toss to coat. Set aside at room temperature.

2. In an extra-large nonstick skillet cook Lebanese Meatballs over medium heat 10 to 12 minutes or until browned and done (160°F), turning occasionally. Serve with tabbouleh. If desired, serve with yogurt.

LEBANESE MEATBALLS: In a bowl combine 1 pound lean ground beef; 2 tablespoons each finely chopped onion and snipped fresh parsley; 1 clove garlic, minced; ½ teaspoon each ground coriander, crushed dried mint, and black pepper; and ¼ teaspoon each ground cumin and salt; mix well. Form mixture into 12 meatballs.

*TIP: Hull-less barley is a heartier form than pearled barley. It still has its bran and germ layers, so it is considered a true whole grain, making it richer in fiber and other nutrients.

Per Serving: 369 cal., 13 g fat (4 g sat. fat), 49 mg chol., 667 mg sodium, 39 g carb., 4 g sugars, 9 g fiber, 25 g pro.

pork and noodle bowl

Prep: 15 minutes   Marinate: 1 hour   Cook: 25 minutes   Makes 4 servings (1½ cups each)

12	ounces boneless pork sirloin chops, cut into thin bite-size strips
½	cup bottled low-fat Asian salad dressing
4	ounces dried multigrain or whole wheat spaghetti
1	tablespoon olive oil
6	cups packaged shredded broccoli slaw mix
¼	cup chopped cashews or sliced almonds, toasted

SIMPLE SWAP

Try packaged cabbage and shredded carrot (coleslaw mix) for the broccoli slaw mix.

1. In a bowl combine pork and ¼ cup of the salad dressing. Cover and marinate at least 1 hour.

2. Cook pasta according to package directions; drain and return to pot. Add the remaining ¼ cup salad dressing, tossing to coat.

3. In an extra-large skillet heat 1½ teaspoons of the olive oil over medium-high heat. Add half of the pork; cook and stir 3 to 4 minutes or until browned and slightly pink in center. Transfer pork to pot with pasta. Repeat with the remaining 1½ teaspoons olive oil and the remaining pork. Toss pork and pasta to combine.

4. Add broccoli slaw mix to hot skillet. Cook and stir about 3 minutes or until just starting to wilt. Transfer to pasta mixture, tossing to combine. Top pasta mixture with cashews.

Per Serving: *313 cal., 8 g fat (1 g sat. fat), 54 mg chol., 544 mg sodium, 33 g carb., 8 g sugars, 6 g fiber, 29 g pro.*

pork loin with parsnips and pears

Start to Finish: 25 minutes   Makes 4 servings (4 to 5 ounces pork and ¾ cup pear mixture each)

- 1½   pounds boneless pork loin
-     Salt and black pepper
- 3   tablespoons Pickapeppa sauce or Worcestershire sauce
- 1   tablespoon olive oil
- 3   to 4 small parsnips, peeled and sliced
- 2   pears, cored and sliced and/or chopped
- ½   cup pear nectar or apple juice
-     Fresh Italian parsley (optional)

SIMPLE SWAP

Sliced carrots can be used in place of the parsnips.

1. Cut pork into ½-inch-thick slices; sprinkle lightly with salt and pepper. Brush with some of the Pickapeppa sauce.

2. In an extra-large skillet brown pork in hot oil over medium heat, turning once. Transfer pork to a plate; cover and keep warm. In the same skillet cook parsnips and pears about 5 minutes or until parsnips are crisp-tender, stirring occasionally. Stir any remaining Pickapeppa sauce and the pear nectar into skillet. Return pork to skillet. Cook about 5 minutes more or until pork is slightly pink in center. Transfer pork and pear mixture to a serving platter. Boil sauce, uncovered, until slightly thickened. Pour over pork and pear mixture. If desired, top with parsley.

Per Serving: *399 cal., 15 g fat (4 g sat. fat), 94 mg chol., 318 mg sodium, 28 g carb., 15 g sugars, 4 g fiber, 38 g pro.*

maple-cider pork with roasted beets and cabbage

Prep: 15 minutes   Cook: 4 minutes   Roast: 45 minutes at 400°F

Makes 4 servings (3½ ounces pork, 1¼ cups cabbage mixture, and ¼ cup sauce each)

- 6   **cups coarsely shredded cabbage**
- 1   **pound yellow or red beets, peeled and coarsley chopped**
- 2   **cups apple cider**
- ½   **teaspoon salt**
- ½   **teaspoon black pepper**
- 1   **tablespoon olive oil**
- 1   **1-pound natural pork tenderloin, trimmed**
- 2   **cups coarsely chopped, peeled tart apples**
- 3   **tablespoons cider vinegar**
- 3   **tablespoons pure maple syrup**

1. Preheat oven to 400°F. In a roasting pan combine the cabbage, beets, apple cider, and ¼ teaspoon each of the salt and pepper; toss to coat. Roast 20 minutes.

2. Meanwhile, sprinkle pork with the remaining ¼ teaspoon each salt and pepper. In a large nonstick skillet cook pork in hot oil over medium-high heat 4 to 5 minutes or until browned on all sides.

3. Remove roasting pan from oven. Add apples; toss to combine. Place pork in roasting pan and continue to roast 25 to 30 minutes or until done (145°F).

4. Transfer meat to a cutting board. Tent with foil; let rest. Using a slotted spoon, transfer cabbage mixture to a serving platter, reserving any remaining pan juices. For sauce, stir vinegar into roasting pan. Place pan over medium-high heat. Bring to boiling; reduce heat. Simmer 5 minutes. Stir in maple syrup. Slice pork and serve with cabbage mixture. Spoon sauce over top.

Per Serving: *342 cal., 6 g fat (1 g sat. fat), 74 mg chol., 444 mg sodium, 46 g carb., 36 g sugars, 6 g fiber, 26 g pro.*

PERFECT PAIR   Boil small red potatoes and toss them with chopped shallots that have been sautéed in a little butter to serve with this saucy dish.

pork tenderloin sandwiches with chimichurri sauce

Prep: 25 minutes   Cook: 5 minutes   Makes 4 servings (1 sandwich each)

1   **pound pork tenderloin, trimmed**
¼   **teaspoon salt**
¼   **teaspoon black pepper**
2   **teaspoons olive oil**
8   **slices whole grain bread, toasted**
4   **leaves green leaf lettuce**
1   **recipe Chimichurri Sauce**
8   **slices tomato**
¼   **cup light mayonnaise (optional)**

1. Cut tenderloin into four equal pieces. Using the flat side of a meat mallet, flatten the tenderloin pieces between two pieces of plastic wrap to about ¼ inch thick. Sprinkle evenly with the salt and pepper.

2. In an extra-large nonstick skillet heat olive oil over medium-high heat. Reduce heat to medium. Cook tenderloin pieces in hot oil 5 to 7 minutes or until just pink inside. Remove from heat.

3. To assemble sandwiches, top four slices of toast with lettuce, tenderloin pieces, Chimichurri Sauce, and tomato slices. If desired, spread remaining toast slices with mayonnaise before adding to sandwiches. Serve immediately.

CHIMICHURRI SAUCE: In a blender or food processor combine 1 cup packed fresh Italian parsley; 2 tablespoons each snipped fresh oregano, finely chopped shallot, red wine vinegar, and lime juice; 1 tablespoon olive oil; 3 cloves garlic, minced; and ½ teaspoon crushed red pepper. Cover and blend until finely chopped, scraping sides as necessary.

Per Serving: *343 cal., 10 g fat (2 g sat. fat), 70 mg chol., 506 mg sodium, 30 g carb., 4 g sugars, 6 g fiber, 32 g pro.*

PERFECT PAIR   These fresh and flavorful sandwiches won't weigh you down at lunch like traditional tenderloin sandwiches. Pair with a vegetable-filled soup to fuel you through the afternoon.

bacon, blue cheese, and pear dinner pie

Prep: 20 minutes   Bake: 15 minutes at 400°F   Makes 4 to 6 servings (1 rectangle each)

- 4   slices lower-sodium, less-fat bacon
- 1   8.5-ounce package corn muffin mix
- ½   cup all-purpose flour
- 2   teaspoons snipped fresh thyme or 1 teaspoon dried thyme, crushed
- 1   egg, lightly beaten
- ¼   cup fat-free milk
- 1   large pear or apple, cored and thinly sliced
- ⅓   cup crumbled blue cheese or shredded cheddar cheese
- ¼   cup chopped toasted walnuts (optional)
      Snipped fresh thyme (optional)

1. Preheat oven to 400°F. Line a 15×10-inch baking pan with parchment paper; set aside. In a large skillet cook bacon over medium heat until crisp. Drain bacon on paper towels, reserving 2 tablespoons of the drippings. Crumble bacon.

2. Meanwhile, for the crust, in a bowl stir together muffin mix, flour, and thyme. Stir in egg and milk. Gather mixture into a ball, kneading gently until it holds together. Using floured hands, press dough into a 12×8-inch rectangle in the prepared baking pan.

3. Arrange pear slices on top of crust. Brush pear slices and crust with 1 to 2 tablespoons of the reserved bacon drippings. Bake 10 minutes. Sprinkle with blue cheese and crumbled bacon. Bake about 5 minutes more or until edges are golden and center is set. If desired, sprinkle with walnuts and additional fresh thyme. Cut into rectangles.

Per Serving: *389 cal., 8 g fat (3 g sat. fat), 59 mg chol., 632 mg sodium, 66 g carb., 16 g sugars, 2 g fiber, 12 g pro.*

PERFECT PAIR   This simple, flavorful savory tart just needs a fresh spinach salad dressed with a light balsamic vinaigrette.

range-top chicken, macaroni, and cheese

Start to Finish: 35 minutes   Makes 5 servings (1⅓ cups each)

1½ cups dried multigrain or regular elbow macaroni
    Nonstick cooking spray
12 ounces skinless, boneless chicken breast halves, cut into 1-inch pieces
¼   cup finely chopped onion
1   6.5-ounce package light semisoft cheese with garlic and fines herbes
1⅔ cups fat-free milk
1   tablespoon all-purpose flour
¾   cup shredded reduced-fat cheddar cheese (3 ounces)
2   cups fresh baby spinach
1   cup cherry tomatoes, quartered

1. Cook macaroni according to package directions; drain.

2. Meanwhile, coat a large nonstick skillet with cooking spray. Heat skillet over medium-high heat. Add chicken and onion; cook 4 to 6 minutes or until chicken is no longer pink and onion is tender, stirring frequently. (If onion browns too quickly, reduce heat to medium.) Remove from heat. Stir in semisoft cheese until melted.

3. In a bowl whisk together milk and flour until smooth. Add all at once to chicken mixture. Cook and stir over medium heat until thickened and bubbly. Reduce heat to low. Gradually stir in cheddar cheese until melted. Add cooked macaroni; cook and stir 1 to 2 minutes or until heated. Stir in spinach. Top with cherry tomatoes.

Per Serving: *369 cal., 12 g fat (7 g sat. fat), 85 mg chol., 393 mg sodium, 33 g carb., 6 g sugars, 4 g fiber, 33 g pro.*

PERFECT PAIR   This rich-tasting dish only needs a simple side of steamed green beans topped with chopped toasted walnuts, lemon zest, and minced garlic.

coconut-curry chicken

Prep: 25 minutes   Cook: 20 minutes   Makes 4 servings (1 cup chicken mixture and ½ cup rice each)

SIMPLE SWAP

Trimmed pork tenderloin is a perfect option to chicken thighs.

Nonstick cooking spray
1 pound skinless, boneless chicken thighs, cut into bite-size pieces
1 15-ounce can unsweetened light coconut milk
2 tablespoons red curry paste
1 tablespoon natural peanut butter
1 tablespoon reduced-sodium soy sauce
2 cups fresh green beans (halved lengthwise if large)
1 medium red sweet pepper, cut into thin strips
2 medium carrots, cut into matchsticks
⅓ cup snipped fresh cilantro
¼ cup sliced green onions
2 cups hot cooked brown rice
Lime wedges

1. Coat an extra-large nonstick skillet with cooking spray. Heat skillet over medium-high heat. Add chicken. Cook until no longer pink, stirring occasionally. Add the next four ingredients (through soy sauce). Stir to combine. Add the next three ingredients (through carrots). Bring to boiling; reduce heat. Simmer, uncovered, 10 to 15 minutes or until vegetables are tender, stirring occasionally. Stir in cilantro and green onions. Serve over rice with lime wedges.

Per Serving: *393 cal., 14 g fat (7 g sat. fat), 106 mg chol., 464 mg sodium, 38 g carb., 8 g sugars, 6 g fiber, 30 g pro.*

chicken and broccolini cavatelli

Prep: 40 minutes   Roast: 20 minutes at 400°F   Makes 6 servings (1 cup each)

1 whole bulb garlic
3 teaspoons olive oil
2 cups dried cavatelli
3 cups Broccolini spears
2 ounces pancetta, finely chopped
1 pound skinless, boneless chicken breast halves, cut into 1½- to 2-inch pieces
3 tablespoons light butter with canola oil
3 tablespoons all-purpose flour
2 tablespoons snipped fresh chives
½ teaspoon salt
¼ teaspoon black pepper
1 cup fat-free milk
½ cup evaporated fat-free milk
2 tablespoons freshly grated Parmesan cheese

SIMPLE SWAP

If you can't find Broccolini, use broccoli florets or cut green beans.

1. Preheat oven to 400°F. Cut off the top ½ inch of the garlic bulb to expose ends of individual cloves. Leaving bulb whole, remove any loose papery outer layers. Place bulb, cut end up, on a double thickness of foil. Drizzle bulb with 1 teaspoon of the olive oil. Bring foil up around bulb and fold edges together to loosely enclose. Roast 20 to 25 minutes or until garlic feels soft when squeezed. Let cool. Squeeze garlic from skins into a small bowl; mash with a fork.

2. Meanwhile, cook pasta according to package directions, adding Broccolini for the last 4 minutes of cooking. Drain, reserving ½ cup of the pasta cooking liquid.

3. In a 6-quart Dutch oven cook pancetta in the remaining 2 teaspoons olive oil over medium heat 5 to 7 minutes or until crisp. Remove pancetta from Dutch oven. Add chicken to Dutch oven. Cook 7 to 8 minutes or until no longer pink. Remove chicken from Dutch oven.

4. In the same Dutch oven melt light butter over medium heat. Whisk in the mashed garlic and the next four ingredients (through pepper) until combined. Whisk in milks until smooth. Cook and stir until thickened and bubbly. Add Parmesan cheese and the cooked chicken, pasta, and Broccolini. Toss to combine. Add the reserved pasta cooking liquid as needed to reach desired consistency. Top with pancetta and additional snipped fresh chives.

Per Serving: *343 cal., 10 g fat (3 g sat. fat), 57 mg chol., 464 mg sodium, 33 g carb., 7 g sugars, 2 g fiber, 27 g pro.*

sweet and tangy chicken wraps

Prep: 20 minutes   Chill: 1 hour   Makes 2 servings (1 wrap each)

¼   **cup plain fat-free Greek yogurt**
1   **tablespoon honey**
¼   **teaspoon black pepper**
⅛   **teaspoon garlic powder**
1½   **cups chopped cooked chicken breast**
1½   **cups baby spinach leaves or mixed baby greens**
2   **8-inch whole wheat tortillas**
2   **tablespoons very thinly sliced red onion**
2   **sweet or dill lengthwise sandwich pickle slices or 8 regular slices**
2   **tablespoons pomegranate seeds (optional)**

SIMPLE SWAP

You can use whole wheat pitas, flatbread, or even crepes for the tortillas.

1. In a bowl stir together the first four ingredients (through garlic powder). Add chicken; toss gently to coat. Cover and chill at least 1 hour.

2. Divide spinach evenly over the top three-fourths of each tortilla. Layer with onion and pickles. Divide chicken mixture between wraps. If desired, sprinkle with pomegranate seeds. Roll up wraps. If desired, cut wraps in half and secure with toothpicks. Serve immediately or wrap tightly in plastic wrap and refrigerate until serving time.

Per Serving: *381 cal., 7 g fat (2 g sat. fat), 95 mg chol., 890 mg sodium, 48 g carb., 11 g sugars, 6 g fiber, 34 g pro.*

open-face philly-style chicken sandwiches

Start to Finish: 30 minutes   Makes 6 servings (1 sandwich each)

1¼ pounds skinless, boneless chicken breast halves, cut into thin strips
 1 tablespoon olive oil
 2 cups thinly sliced onion
 1 cup green, red, and/or yellow sweet pepper strips
 1 to 2 cloves garlic, minced
 1 teaspoon dried Italian seasoning, crushed
 ½ teaspoon black pepper
 4 ounces reduced-fat provolone cheese, shredded
 6 ½-inch-thick slices whole grain bread

1. Preheat broiler. In a large skillet cook chicken in hot oil over medium-high heat about 5 minutes or until no longer pink, stirring occasionally. Reduce heat to medium. Add the next five ingredients (through black pepper). Cook and stir 5 to 8 minutes or until vegetables are tender. Reduce heat to low. Sprinkle shredded cheese over the chicken mixture. Cover and cook about 1 minute more or until the cheese is melted.

2. Meanwhile, arrange the bread on a baking sheet. Broil bread 4 to 5 inches from the heat 1 to 2 minutes per side or until toasted. Transfer portions of cheese-topped chicken mixture onto toasted bread slices.

Per Serving: *321 cal., 10 g fat (3 g sat. fat), 71 mg chol., 435 mg sodium, 26 g carb., 6 g sugars, 5 g fiber, 31 g pro.*

PERFECT PAIR   Serve crisp tart apple slices and a few toasted whole walnuts with these sandwiches to make a satisfying lunch.

chicken soup with chive dumplings

Prep: 45 minutes   Cook: 37 minutes   Makes 6 servings (¾ cup soup and 1 dumpling each)

1	pound skinless, boneless chicken breast halves
	Black pepper
2	tablespoons olive oil
1	cup chopped carrots
1	cup chopped celery
⅓	cup chopped leek
6	cups reduced-sodium chicken broth
4	sprigs fresh thyme
1	bay leaf
¼	teaspoon salt
1½	cups all-purpose flour
1	tablespoon snipped fresh chives
2	teaspoons baking powder
½	teaspoon salt
3	tablespoons cold butter, cut up
¾	cup milk
¼	cup snipped fresh Italian parsley

SIMPLE SWAP

Go vegetarian with vegetable broth for the chicken broth and no chicken.

1. Sprinkle chicken with pepper. In a 4- to 5-quart Dutch oven cook chicken in hot oil over medium-high heat until browned, turning once. Reduce heat to medium. Cook, covered, 7 to 9 minutes or until chicken is no longer pink (165°F). Remove chicken from pan.

2. Add carrots, celery, and leek to Dutch oven. Cook, covered, 5 to 7 minutes or until vegetables are tender, stirring occasionally.

3. Cut chicken into ½-inch pieces. Return chicken to Dutch oven. Add broth, thyme, bay leaf, and the ¼ teaspoon salt. Bring to boiling; reduce heat. Simmer, uncovered, 15 minutes.

4. Meanwhile, for dumplings, in a bowl stir together the next four ingredients (through ½ teaspoon salt). Using a pastry blender, cut in butter until mixture resembles coarse crumbs. Stir in milk just until combined.

5. Remove and discard thyme and bay leaf from soup. Stir in parsley. Bring to boiling. Drop dumpling dough by large spoonfuls onto bubbling soup to make six dumplings. Cook, uncovered, 10 minutes. Reduce heat to medium-low. Cook, covered, about 10 minutes more or until a toothpick inserted in centers of dumplings comes out clean.

TO MAKE AHEAD: Prepare as directed through Step 3. Cover and chill up to 3 days. To serve, bring soup to boiling. Continue as directed.

Per Serving: *337 cal., 13 g fat (5 g sat. fat), 73 mg chol., 648 mg sodium, 30 g carb., 3 g sugars, 2 g fiber, 24 g pro.*

succotash salad with buttermilk-avocado dressing

Prep: 25 minutes   Cook: 20 minutes
Makes 4 servings (1⅓ cups salad and about 3 tablespoons dressing each)

SIMPLE SWAP

Use 1 cup frozen whole kernel corn and/or frozen lima beans for the fresh; cook according to package directions.

2   ears fresh sweet corn
1   cup fresh lima beans
1   large head butterhead (Boston or Bibb) lettuce, torn
2   cups sliced grilled chicken breast*
6   slices lower-sodium, less-fat bacon, crisp-cooked and crumbled
½   cup finely chopped red onion
½   cup crumbled blue cheese or feta cheese (2 ounces)
1   recipe Buttermilk-Avocado Dressing

1. Cut corn kernels from cobs; discard cobs. In a small saucepan bring 1 cup lightly salted water to boiling. Add lima beans; simmer about 15 minutes or until tender. Remove with a slotted spoon. Add corn to water. Simmer about 3 minutes or until tender; drain.

2. Line a large platter or four plates with the lettuce. Arrange the next four ingredients (through cheese) and the corn and lima beans in rows on lettuce. Serve with Buttermilk-Avocado Dressing.

BUTTERMILK-AVOCADO DRESSING: In a blender combine ¾ cup buttermilk; half of an avocado, peeled and seeded; 1 tablespoon snipped fresh Italian parsley; ¼ teaspoon each onion powder, dry mustard, salt, and black pepper; and 1 clove garlic, minced. Cover and blend until smooth.

*TO GRILL CHICKEN: Lightly season 12 ounces skinless, boneless chicken breast halves with salt and black pepper. Grill chicken, covered, over medium heat 12 to 15 minutes or until chicken is no longer pink (165°F), turning once.

Per Serving: *345 cal., 13 g fat (5 g sat. fat), 82 mg chol., 609 mg sodium, 24 g carb., 7 g sugars, 5 g fiber, 33 g pro.*

mexican black bean and chicken platter

Start to Finish: 30 minutes   Makes 6 servings (about 2 cups each)

¼ cup cider vinegar

3 tablespoons olive oil or vegetable oil

3 tablespoons snipped fresh cilantro

1 canned chipotle chile pepper in adobo sauce, drained and finely chopped*

1 clove garlic, minced

½ teaspoon salt

1 15-ounce can black beans, rinsed and drained

¾ cup cooked fresh or frozen whole kernel corn

½ cup chopped orange or yellow sweet pepper (optional)

3½ cups shredded cooked chicken

10 grape tomatoes, halved

¼ cup sliced green onions

10 cups coarsely shredded lettuce

1 avocado, halved, seeded, peeled, and sliced (optional)

1 lime, halved and cut into wedges

1. For dressing, in a screw-top jar combine the first six ingredients (through salt). Cover and shake well. For relish, in a bowl combine black beans, corn, and, if desired, sweet pepper. Drizzle with 2 tablespoons of the dressing; toss gently to coat. In another bowl toss together chicken and 1 tablespoon of the dressing. In a third bowl combine tomatoes and green onions.

2. Line a large serving platter with shredded lettuce. Arrange tomato mixture, relish, chicken mixture, and, if desired, avocado slices in rows on top of lettuce. Drizzle with the remaining dressing. Serve with lime wedges.

*TIP: Chile peppers contain oils that can irritate your skin and eyes. Wear plastic or rubber gloves when working with them.

TO MAKE AHEAD: Prepare salad as directed, except toss avocado slices with 1 tablespoon lime juice to prevent browning and do not drizzle salad with dressing. Cover and chill salad and dressing separately up to 1 hour. Before serving, drizzle salad with the remaining dressing.

Per Serving: *319 cal., 14 g fat (3 g sat. fat), 73 mg chol., 533 mg sodium, 22 g carb., 5 g sugars, 6 g fiber, 30 g pro.*

PERFECT PAIR   Complete this feast with a stack of warmed corn tortillas as a serve-along.

bow tie pesto alfredo

Start to Finish: 25 minutes   Makes 4 servings (1½ cups each)

SIMPLE SWAP

Use 6 ounces shredded cooked chicken breast for the chicken sausage.

- 3 **cups dried multigrain bow tie pasta**
- 1 **cup frozen peas**
  Nonstick cooking spray
- ½ **of a 12-ounce package cooked smoked chicken sausage with apple, halved lengthwise and sliced**
- 2 **teaspoons olive oil**
- 2 **cups sliced fresh mushrooms**
- ¾ **cup chopped red sweet pepper**
- 1 **cup light Alfredo pasta sauce**
- 1 **tablespoon basil pesto**
- ⅛ **to ¼ teaspoon crushed red pepper**
- 1 **tablespoon finely shredded Romano or Parmesan cheese (optional)**

1. Cook pasta according to package directions, adding frozen peas the last 1 minute of cooking; drain. Return pasta mixture to hot pan; cover and keep warm.

2. Meanwhile, coat a large nonstick skillet with cooking spray; heat skillet over medium-high heat. Add sausage; cook about 3 minutes or until browned, stirring occasionally. Remove sausage from skillet; keep warm. Add oil to the skillet. Add mushrooms and sweet pepper; cook 5 to 7 minutes or until tender, stirring occasionally. Return sausage to skillet. Stir in Alfredo sauce, pesto, and crushed red pepper; heat.

3. Add sausage mixture to cooked pasta mixture; stir gently to coat. If desired, sprinkle with cheese.

Per Serving: *385 cal., 15 g fat (5 g sat. fat), 56 mg chol., 665 mg sodium, 45 g carb., 11 g sugars, 6 g fiber, 20 g pro.*

almond noodle bowl

Start to Finish: 30 minutes   Makes 5 servings (1¼ cups each)

- 1   teaspoon toasted sesame oil
- 4   cloves garlic, minced
- ¼   teaspoon crushed red pepper (optional)
- ¼   cup almond butter
- ¼   cup canned unsweetened light coconut milk
- 1   tablespoon lime juice
- 1   tablespoon reduced-sodium soy sauce
- ½   teaspoon ground ginger
- 4   ounces dried whole grain spaghetti
- 1   tablespoon olive oil
- 1   pound skinless, boneless chicken breast halves, cut into 1-inch pieces
- 1   16-ounce package frozen stir-fry vegetables
- 2   tablespoons water
- ¼   cup fresh cilantro leaves
- 2   tablespoons chopped dry-roasted whole almonds

SIMPLE SWAP

Add more Asian flavor with soba noodles instead of spaghetti.

1. For sauce, in a small skillet heat sesame oil over medium heat. Add garlic and, if desired, crushed red pepper; cook and stir about 1 minute or until garlic starts to brown. Stir in almond butter until melted. Stir in the next four ingredients (through ginger). Remove from heat.

2. Cook spaghetti according to package directions; drain.

3. Meanwhile, in a large skillet heat olive oil over medium-high heat. Add chicken; cook and stir 4 to 5 minutes or until no longer pink. Stir in vegetables and the water. Cook, covered, about 5 minutes or until vegetables are crisp-tender, stirring occasionally. Stir in sauce and spaghetti. Sprinkle with cilantro and almonds.

Per Serving: *359 cal., 16 g fat (2 g sat. fat), 58 mg chol., 280 mg sodium, 27 g carb., 4 g sugars, 5 g fiber, 27 g pro.*

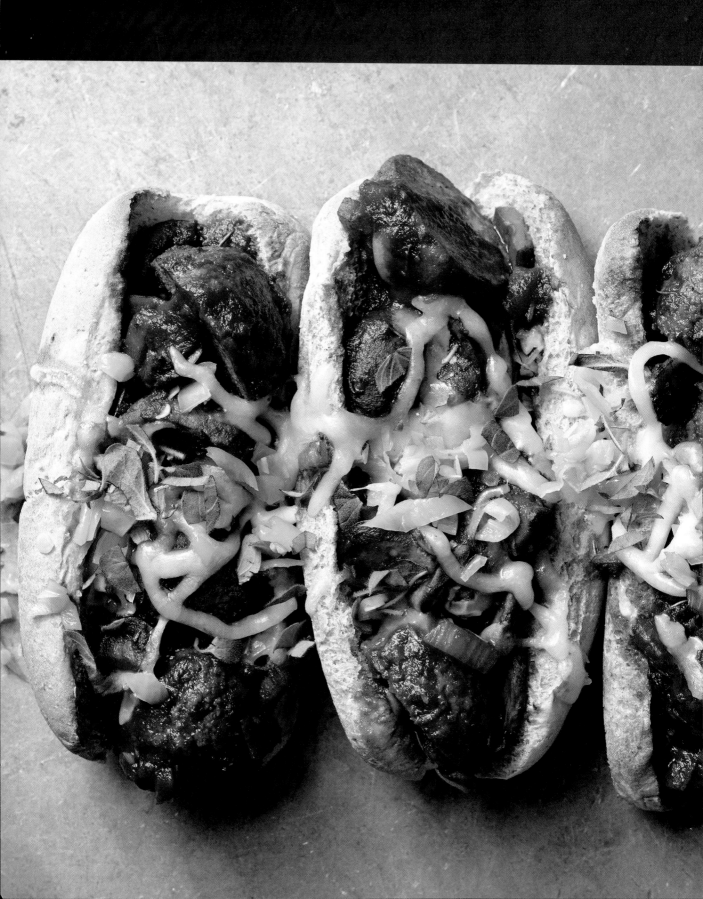

italian meatball rolls

Start to Finish: 30 minutes   Makes 4 servings (1 sandwich each)

Nonstick cooking spray
2½ cups thinly sliced fresh cremini mushrooms
½ cup chopped onion
2 cloves garlic, minced
1 8-ounce can no-salt-added tomato sauce
2 tablespoons balsamic vinegar
½ teaspoon dried rosemary, crushed
½ teaspoon dried oregano, crushed
8 ounces refrigerated Italian-style cooked turkey meatballs (8 meatballs), halved if desired
4 whole wheat hot dog buns, split
¼ cup finely shredded reduced-fat mozzarella cheese (1 ounce)
Snipped fresh oregano (optional)

SIMPLE SWAP

Go open-face. Halve two mini baguettes lengthwise and top as directed.

1. Preheat broiler. Coat a large nonstick skillet with cooking spray; heat skillet over medium heat. Cook mushrooms, onion, and garlic in hot skillet 5 to 10 minutes or until tender, stirring occasionally. Stir in the next four ingredients (through dried oregano). Bring to boiling; reduce heat. Simmer, covered, 2 minutes. Stir in meatballs. Simmer, covered, about 5 minutes more or until meatballs are heated.

2. Meanwhile, open buns so they lie flat and place on a baking sheet. Broil 4 to 5 inches from the heat about 1 minute or until lightly toasted. Divide meatball mixture among buns; sprinkle with cheese. Broil 1 to 2 minutes more or until cheese is melted. If desired, sprinkle with fresh oregano.

Per Serving: *320 cal., 11 g fat (3 g sat. fat), 65 mg chol., 605 mg sodium, 36 g carb., 9 g sugars, 4 g fiber, 19 g pro.*

indian-spiced turkey kabob pitas

Prep: 25 minutes   Grill: 8 minutes   Makes 4 servings (1 sandwich each)

1	teaspoon whole cumin seeds
1	cup shredded cucumber
⅓	cup seeded and chopped roma tomato
¼	cup slivered red onion
¼	cup shredded radishes
¼	cup snipped fresh cilantro
¼	teaspoon black pepper
1	pound turkey breast, cut into 1-inch cubes
1	recipe Curry Blend
¼	cup plain fat-free Greek yogurt
4	2-ounce whole wheat pita bread rounds

SIMPLE SWAP

Use chicken breast or turkey thigh meat for the turkey breast.

1. If using wooden skewers, soak in water 30 minutes. In a small dry skillet toast cumin seeds over medium heat about 1 minute or until fragrant. Transfer to a bowl. Add the next six ingredients (through pepper) to bowl; stir to combine.

2. In another bowl combine turkey and Curry Blend; stir to coat. Thread turkey cubes evenly onto skewers. Grill kabobs, uncovered, over medium heat 8 to 12 minutes or until turkey is no longer pink, turning kabobs occasionally.

3. Remove turkey from skewers. Spread Greek yogurt evenly on pita rounds. Using a slotted spoon, spoon cucumber mixture over yogurt. Top with grilled turkey.

CURRY BLEND: In a bowl stir together 2 teaspoons olive oil; 1 teaspoon curry powder; ½ teaspoon each ground cumin, ground turmeric, and ground coriander; ¼ teaspoon ground ginger; ⅛ teaspoon salt; and ⅛ teaspoon cayenne pepper.

Per Serving: *322 cal., 5 g fat (1 g sat. fat), 70 mg chol., 442 mg sodium, 35 g carb., 2 g sugars, 5 g fiber, 35 g pro.*

italian barley and sausage casseroles

Prep: 45 minutes Bake: 40 minutes at 350°F Makes 4 servings (1 casserole each)

Nonstick cooking spray

4 ounces uncooked bulk turkey Italian sausage or smoked turkey Italian sausage link, halved lengthwise and thinly sliced

3 cups sliced fresh button mushrooms

½ cup chopped onion

2 cloves garlic, minced

2 cups cooked barley*

1½ cups no-salt-added tomato pasta sauce

1½ cups shredded part-skim mozzarella cheese (6 ounces)

½ cup bottled roasted red sweet pepper, chopped

¼ cup pitted green olives, chopped

2 tablespoons snipped fresh basil

½ cup red and/or yellow grape or cherry tomatoes, halved

1. Preheat oven to 350°F. Coat four 12- to 14-ounce individual casseroles with cooking spray. Coat a large nonstick skillet with cooking spray. Heat skillet over medium heat. Add sausage, mushrooms, onion, and garlic. Cook 8 to 10 minutes or until bulk sausage (if using) is no longer pink and vegetables are tender. Drain off fat.

2. Stir barley, pasta sauce, 1 cup of the cheese, the roasted pepper, olives, and 1 tablespoon of the basil into skillet. Divide sausage mixture among the prepared casseroles. Cover with foil.

3. Bake 30 minutes. Sprinkle with the remaining ½ cup cheese. Bake, uncovered, about 10 minutes more or until heated and cheese is melted. Top with tomatoes and the remaining 1 tablespoon basil.

*TIP: For 2 cups cooked quick-cooking barley, in a medium saucepan bring 1⅓ cups water to boiling; stir in ¾ cup quick-cooking barley. Return to boiling; reduce heat. Simmer, covered, 10 to 12 minutes or until barley is tender; drain. For 2 cups cooked regular barley, prepare as directed, except use 2 cups water and ½ cup regular barley; simmer, covered, about 45 minutes.

Per Serving: *346 cal., 13 g fat (6 g sat. fat), 42 mg chol., 704 mg sodium, 40 g carb., 9 g sugars, 7 g fiber, 20 g pro.*

PERFECT PAIR These individual casseroles go well with a crisp green salad topped with slivered red onion, sweet pepper strips, shaved Parmesan, and an Italian vinaigrette.

tomato-basil turkey burgers

Start to Finish: 30 minutes   Makes 8 servings (1 burger each)

- 2 pounds ground turkey breast
- 2 tablespoons snipped fresh basil
- 2 tablespoons finely chopped oil-packed dried tomatoes
- 1 teaspoon salt
- ½ teaspoon black pepper
- 4 ounces smoked or fresh mozzarella cheese, thinly sliced
- 8 sourdough or other hamburger buns, split and toasted
- 2 cups lightly packed arugula or watercress
- 1 recipe Pesto Mayonnaise (optional)
- 1 yellow sweet pepper, roasted and cut into strips,* or ¾ cup bottled roasted red sweet pepper strips (optional)

1. In a large bowl combine the first five ingredients (through black pepper); mix well. Shape turkey mixture into eight ½-inch-thick patties. Grill burgers, covered, over medium heat 10 to 13 minutes or until done (165°F), turning once and adding cheese the last 1 to 2 minutes of grilling.

2. Serve burgers in buns with arugula and, if desired, Pesto Mayonnaise and roasted pepper strips.

PESTO MAYONNASIE: In a bowl stir together ½ cup light mayonnaise and 2 to 4 tablespoons basil pesto.

*TIP: To roast sweet peppers on the grill, quarter peppers lengthwise; remove stems, seeds, and membranes. Grill pepper quarters, skin sides down, covered, over medium heat about 10 minutes or until peppers are charred and very tender. Wrap peppers in foil; let stand about 15 minutes or until cool enough to handle. Peel off and discard skins. Cut peppers into strips.

TO MAKE AHEAD: Prepare patties as directed in Step 1. Cover and chill burgers up to 8 hours. If desired, prepare Pesto Mayonnaise and roasted sweet peppers; cover and chill up to 1 day.

Per Serving: *328 cal., 5 g fat (2 g sat. fat), 65 mg chol., 700 mg sodium, 33 g carb., 2 g sugars, 2 g fiber, 35 g pro.*

PERFECT PAIR   For a refreshing fruit salad, serve burgers with chunks of cantaloupe and honeydew melons splashed with white balsamic vinegar and drizzled with honey.

scallop, mushroom, and fennel campanelle

Start to Finish: 40 minutes   Makes 4 servings (1½ cups each)

8	ounces fresh or frozen sea scallops
2¼	cups dried campanelle pasta
¼	teaspoon salt
¼	teaspoon black pepper
3	teaspoons olive oil
2	cups fresh oyster mushrooms, cut into 2-inch pieces
2	cloves garlic, minced
2	cups chopped kale
1½	cups thinly sliced fennel
¼	cup dry white wine
¼	cup light butter with canola oil
2	tablespoons snipped fresh parsley
2	tablespoons lemon juice
⅛	teaspoon salt

SIMPLE SWAP

Oyster mushrooms can be hard to find. Use any variety of fresh mushroom or even basic button mushrooms.

1. Thaw scallops, if frozen. Rinse scallops and pat dry with paper towels. Cook pasta according to package directions; drain.

2. Sprinkle scallops with the ¼ teaspoon salt and the pepper. In a large nonstick skillet heat 1 teaspoon of the olive oil over medium heat. Add scallops; cook 2 to 4 minutes or until scallops are opaque, turning once. Remove from skillet; keep warm. Add another 1 teaspoon of the oil, the mushrooms, and garlic to the skillet. Cook about 4 minutes or until mushrooms are tender, stirring occasionally. Remove from skillet; keep warm. Add the remaining 1 teaspoon oil, the kale, and fennel. Cook about 7 minutes more or just until kale and fennel are tender.

3. Remove skillet from heat and add the wine. Return to heat. Stir in the remaining ingredients. Add the cooked pasta and the mushroom mixture to the skillet; toss to combine. Cook until heated. Spoon pasta mixture onto plates. Top with scallops.

Per Serving: *331 cal., 10 g fat (3 g sat. fat), 19 mg chol., 567 mg sodium, 42 g carb., 3 g sugars, 4 g fiber, 16 g pro.*

tarragon shrimp with easy risotto

Start to Finish: 40 minutes   Makes 4 servings (6 shrimp and ¾ cup risotto each)

- 1 **pound fresh or frozen large shrimp in shells**
- 1 **tablespoon lemon juice**
- 1 **tablespoon olive oil**
- 3 **cloves garlic, minced**
- 1 teaspoon dried tarragon, crushed
- ¼ **teaspoon salt**
- 1 **tablespoon butter**
- ⅓ **cup chopped onion**
- ⅔ **cup uncooked Arborio rice**
- 1 **14.5-ounce can reduced-sodium chicken broth**
- 1 **cup frozen peas, thawed**
- ¼ **cup grated Parmesan cheese**
  Lemon wedges (optional)

SIMPLE SWAP

Not a fan of tarragon? Use 1 teaspoon dried oregano or thyme in its place.

1. Thaw shrimp, if frozen. Peel and devein shrimp, leaving tails intact. Rinse shrimp; pat dry with paper towels. Place shrimp in a resealable plastic bag set in a shallow dish. For marinade, in a bowl combine the next five ingredients (through salt). Pour marinade over shrimp. Seal bag; turn to coat shrimp. Marinate in the refrigerator 15 to 30 minutes.

2. Meanwhile, in a medium saucepan melt butter over medium heat. Add onion; cook about 5 minutes or until tender, stirring occasionally. Add rice; cook and stir 2 minutes more. Carefully stir in broth. Bring to boiling; reduce heat. Simmer, uncovered, 15 minutes or until rice is tender but firm and risotto is creamy. Remove from heat. Stir in peas. Let stand for 1 minute. Stir in Parmesan cheese.

3. Heat an extra-large skillet over medium heat. Add shrimp and marinade to skillet. Cook about 3 minutes or until shrimp are opaque, stirring frequently. Serve shrimp with risotto. If desired, garnish with lemon wedges.

TO GRILL SHRIMP: Drain shrimp, reserving marinade. Thread shrimp onto metal skewers, leaving ¼ inch between shrimp. Brush shrimp with the reserved marinade. Grill kabobs, covered, over medium-high heat 4 to 6 minutes or until shrimp are opaque, turning once.

Per Serving: *308 cal., 8 g fat (3 g sat. fat), 171 mg chol., 643 mg sodium, 32 g carb., 3 g sugars, 2 g fiber, 27 g pro.*

skewered shrimp and tomato linguine

Start to Finish: 40 minutes   Makes 4 servings (1¼ cups each)

12	ounces fresh or frozen large shrimp
24	red and/or yellow cherry or grape tomatoes
1	tablespoon olive oil
1	clove garlic, minced
¼	teaspoon black pepper
⅛	teaspoon salt
6	ounces dried whole grain linguine
1	tablespoon butter
1	tablespoon lemon juice
4	cups torn baby arugula
1	tablespoon snipped fresh oregano
¼	cup finely shredded Parmesan cheese
	Freshly cracked black pepper
	Lemon wedges (optional)

SIMPLE SWAP

Fresh baby spinach works well as a stand-in for baby arugula.

1. Thaw shrimp, if frozen. If necessary, peel and devein shrimp. Rinse shrimp and pat dry with paper towels. Thread shrimp and tomatoes onto four 10-inch metal skewers. In a bowl whisk together the next four ingredients (through salt). Brush over shrimp and tomatoes. Grill skewers, uncovered, over medium heat 5 to 8 minutes or until shrimp turn opaque, turning once.

2. Meanwhile, prepare linguine according to package directions. Drain, reserving ⅓ cup of the cooking water. Return pasta to pot. Add butter and lemon juice; toss to combine. Add the reserved pasta cooking water, the grilled shrimp and tomatoes, arugula, and oregano. Toss to combine. Sprinkle with Parmesan cheese and cracked black pepper. If desired, serve with lemon wedges.

Per Serving: 321 cal., 10 g fat (3 g sat. fat), 118 mg chol., 603 mg sodium, 40 g carb., 5 g sugars, 7 g fiber, 20 g pro.

pacific salmon paella

Start to Finish: 45 minutes   Makes 6 servings (1½ cups each)

SIMPLE SWAP

Tuna, halibut, or cod can stand in for the salmon.

1¼ pounds fresh or frozen skinless salmon fillets, about 1 inch thick
4 slices applewood-smoked bacon
3 cups sliced fresh cremini or button mushrooms
1 cup chopped onion
2 cloves garlic, minced
2½ cups chicken broth
1 cup uncooked long grain white rice
2 teaspoons snipped fresh thyme or ½ teaspoon dried thyme, crushed
¼ teaspoon cracked black pepper
1 pound fresh asparagus, trimmed and cut into 1-inch pieces, or one 10-ounce package frozen cut asparagus, thawed
⅓ cup chopped roma tomato

1. Thaw salmon, if frozen. Rinse fish and pat dry with paper towels. Cut fish into 1-inch pieces. In a large deep skillet or paella pan cook bacon over medium heat until crisp. Drain bacon on paper towels, reserving drippings in skillet. Crumble bacon.

2. Add mushrooms, onion, and garlic to the reserved drippings in skillet. Cook about 5 minutes or until onion is tender. Stir in broth, rice, and thyme. Bring to boiling; reduce heat. Simmer, covered, 10 minutes.

3. Sprinkle salmon with pepper; toss gently to coat. Place fish and asparagus on top of rice mixture. Simmer, covered, 10 to 12 minutes or until fish flakes easily and asparagus is crisp-tender. Sprinkle with tomato and crumbled bacon.

Per Serving: *313 cal., 9 g fat (2 g sat. fat), 60 mg chol., 498 mg sodium, 32 g carb., 4 g sugars, 2 g fiber, 26 g pro.*

fish tacos with cabbage and chile pepper slaw

Prep: 40 minutes   Bake: 10 minutes at 400°F   Makes 6 servings (2 tacos each)

1½ pounds fresh or frozen cod or halibut fillets	½ teaspoon orange zest
2 tomatillos, husked and cut into ½-inch pieces (2 cups)	½ teaspoon lime zest
2 teaspoons olive oil	Salt and black pepper
1 clove garlic, minced	12 6-inch corn tortillas, warmed*
	1 recipe Cabbage and Chile Pepper Slaw

1. Thaw fish, if frozen. Rinse fish; pat dry with paper towels. Cut fish into 1-inch pieces. Preheat oven to 400°F. In a bowl toss together fish and the next five ingredients (through lime zest). Season with salt and black pepper; set aside.

2. Cut six 12-inch-square pieces of foil. Divide fish mixture among foil squares. Fold foil diagonally in half to form a triangle. Fold edges two or three times to make a packet. Place packets in a single layer on a large baking sheet. Bake 10 to 12 minutes or until packets puff slightly. Carefully open a packet to check fish doneness; fish should flake easily.

3. Divide fish mixture among warm tortillas. Top with Cabbage and Chile Pepper Slaw.

CABBAGE AND CHILE PEPPER SLAW: In a bowl whisk together 3 tablespoons olive oil, 2 tablespoons lime juice, 1 tablespoon orange juice, and salt to taste. Add 1¼ cups thinly shredded green cabbage; ½ cup thinly sliced red onion; ½ cup shredded carrot; 1 poblano or pasilla chile pepper, halved crosswise, seeded, and thinly sliced;** and ¼ cup chopped fresh cilantro. Toss to coat.

*TIP: To warm tortillas, stack tortillas and wrap in microwave-safe paper towels. Microwave about 1 minute or until heated.

**TIP: Chile peppers contain oils that can irritate your skin and eyes. Wear plastic or rubber gloves when working with them.

Per Serving: *341 cal., 13 g fat (2 g sat. fat), 36 mg chol., 293 mg sodium, 30 g carb., 3 g sugars, 5 g fiber, 28 g pro.*

PERFECT PAIR   Serve these tangy tacos with creamy fat-free refried black beans sprinkled with shredded reduced-fat Monterey Jack cheese and sliced green onions.

citrus salsa salmon

Prep: 20 minutes   Broil: 8 minutes   Makes 4 servings (1 salmon fillet and ¾ cup salsa each)

- 4   4- to 5-ounce fresh or frozen skinless salmon fillets, ¾ to 1 inch thick
- ¼   teaspoon salt
- ⅛   teaspoon black pepper
- ¼   cup red jalapeño jelly
- 2   medium oranges, peeled, seeded, and coarsely chopped
- 1   medium grapefruit, peeled and sectioned
- 1   cup grape or cherry tomatoes, halved
-     Salad greens (optional)

SIMPLE SWAP

Use blood oranges instead of regular oranges in the salsa for their unusual color and citrus-berry flavor.

1. Thaw salmon, if frozen. Preheat broiler. Rinse fish and pat dry with paper towels. Sprinkle salmon with salt and pepper. In a small saucepan melt jelly over low heat. Brush 2 tablespoons of the melted jelly over salmon. Set remaining jelly aside.

2. Place salmon on the unheated rack of a broiler pan. Broil 4 inches from the heat 8 to 10 minutes or until fish flakes easily when tested with a fork.

3. Meanwhile, for citrus salsa, in a bowl combine chopped oranges, grapefruit sections, tomatoes, and the remaining melted jelly. Season to taste with additional salt and pepper. Serve with salmon. If desired, garnish with salad greens.

Per Serving: *357 cal., 15 g fat (3 g sat. fat), 62 mg chol., 221 mg sodium, 31 g carb., 22 g sugars, 3 g fiber, 25 g pro.*

spicy oven-baked fish and sweet potato fries

Prep: 20 minutes   Bake: 20 minutes at 425°F   Makes 4 servings (2 pieces fish and 4 ounces chips each)

- 1   pound fresh or frozen white fish fillets, about ½ inch thick
  Nonstick cooking spray
- 1   pound sweet potatoes, cut into ¼- to ½-inch sticks
- 1   tablespoon olive oil
- 2½ teaspoons chili powder
- 1   teaspoon Old Bay seasoning or seafood seasoning

- ½   teaspoon salt
- ⅓   cup milk
- ⅓   cup all-purpose flour
- ⅓   cup fine dry bread crumbs
- 1   teaspoon paprika
- ¼   teaspoon black pepper
- 2   tablespoons butter, melted
  Lemon wedges and/or fresh parsley (optional)

1. Thaw fish, if frozen. Rinse fish; pat dry with paper towels. Cut fish into 3×2-inch pieces. Cover and chill until needed.

2. Preheat oven to 425°F. Line a large baking sheet with foil; lightly coat with cooking spray. For fries, pat potatoes dry with paper towels; place in a large bowl. Add the olive oil, ½ teaspoon of the chili powder, the Old Bay seasoning, and ¼ teaspoon of the salt. Toss to coat. Arrange potatoes in a single layer on one half of the prepared baking sheet. Bake 10 minutes.

3. Meanwhile, for fish, place milk in a shallow dish. Place flour in another shallow dish. In a third shallow dish combine bread crumbs, the remaining 2 teaspoons chili powder, the paprika, the remaining ¼ teaspoon salt, and the pepper. Stir in melted butter until combined.

4. Dip fish pieces in milk; coat with flour. Dip again in the milk, then in the bread crumb mixture. Remove baking sheet from oven. Carefully turn potatoes over. Place fish on the other half of the hot baking sheet; return to oven. Bake 10 to 15 minutes more or until potatoes are golden brown and fish flakes easily. If desired, serve fish with lemon wedges and/or fresh parsley.

Per Serving: *384 cal., 13 g fat (5 g sat. fat), 74 mg chol., 785 mg sodium, 40 g carb., 7 g sugars, 5 g fiber, 28 g pro.*

PERFECT PAIR   Toss broccoli slaw mix with a light coleslaw dressing. Squeeze some of the lemon wedges over for a crunchy, tangy accompaniment to the fish.

almond-coated cod with cabbage-fennel slaw

Prep: 20 minutes   Bake: 4 minutes at 425°F   Makes 4 servings (1 fish fillet and 1¼ cups slaw each)

4	4- to 5-ounce fresh or frozen skinless cod fillets	¼	teaspoon black pepper
1	medium fennel bulb	4	cups shredded savoy or white cabbage
1	lemon	1	medium orange, peeled and cut into segments**
2	tablespoons olive oil		Nonstick cooking spray
1	tablespoon honey	2	tablespoons honey mustard
1	teaspoon orange zest*	½	cup finely chopped almonds
¼	teaspoon salt		

1. Thaw fish, if frozen. Snip 2 tablespoons fennel fronds. Reserve additional fronds for garnish. Trim and discard fennel stalk and any damaged outer layer from bulb. Cut bulb in half lengthwise; remove and discard core. Thinly slice bulb.

2. Remove 1 teaspoon zest and squeeze 3 tablespoons juice from lemon. In a bowl whisk together lemon zest and peel and the next five ingredients (through pepper). Add sliced fennel, the 2 tablespoons snipped fennel fronds, and cabbage. Toss to combine. Gently stir in orange segments.

3. Preheat oven to 425°F. Line a large baking sheet with foil; coat foil with cooking spray. Measure thickness of fish. Arrange fish on prepared baking sheet. Brush tops of fish with mustard. Sprinkle almonds over fish, pressing onto fish to adhere. Lightly coat tops of fish with cooking spray. Bake 4 to 6 minutes per ½-inch thickness or until fish flakes easily. Serve with slaw. Top with additional reserved fennel fronds.

*TIP: Before peeling and sectioning the orange, remove 1 teaspoon zest from it.

**TIP: To section the orange, cut a thin slice from both ends using a paring knife. Place the flat end of the orange on a cutting board. Use the knife to cut away the peel and white pith from top to bottom. To remove sections, hold the orange over the slaw bowl. Cut toward the center of the orange between one section and the membrane, then cut out along the membrane on the other side of the section to free each section. Let sections and any juice fall into bowl.

Per Serving: 331 cal., 14 g fat (2 g sat. fat), 61 mg chol., 318 mg sodium, 22 g carb., 13 g sugars, 6 g fiber, 30 g pro.

PERFECT PAIR   Complete this meal with vitamin-packed sweet potato fries. Toss thin wedges of sweet potato with a little olive oil, salt, and black pepper. Roast in a baking pan in a 425°F oven about 20 minutes or until lightly browned.

manhattan clam chowder

Start to Finish: 40 minutes   Makes 4 servings (2 cups each)

- 1 cup chopped celery
- ⅓ cup chopped onion
- ¼ cup chopped carrot
- 2 tablespoons olive oil or vegetable oil
- 2 cups reduced-sodium chicken broth
- 1 8-ounce bottle clam juice or 1 cup reduced-sodium chicken broth
- 2 cups cubed red-skin potatoes
- ¼ cup no-salt-added tomato paste
- 1 teaspoon dried thyme, crushed
- ⅛ teaspoon cayenne pepper
- ⅛ teaspoon black pepper
- 4 6.5-ounce cans minced clams, drained
- 1 14.5-ounce can no-salt-added diced tomatoes, undrained
- ¼ cup broken crisp-cooked bacon* or purchased cooked bacon pieces

1. In a large saucepan cook celery, onion, and carrot in hot oil over medium heat until tender, stirring occasionally. Stir in the 2 cups broth and clam juice. Stir in the next five ingredients (through black pepper). Bring to boiling; reduce heat. Simmer, covered, 10 to 12 minutes or until potatoes are tender. Stir in clams and tomatoes. Top with bacon.

*TIP: If you prefer to cook your own bacon, cook four slices, reserving 2 tablespoons drippings. Omit oil. Cook the celery, onion, and carrot in the reserved drippings.

TO MAKE AHEAD: Prepare as directed. Cool soup slightly and transfer to an airtight container. Cover and chill up to 3 days or freeze up to 2 months. If frozen, thaw soup in the refrigerator. Heat soup in a large saucepan over medium heat, stirring occasionally.

Per Serving: *308 cal., 11 g fat (2 g sat. fat), 43 mg chol., 663 mg sodium, 28 g carb., 8 g sugars, 5 g fiber, 25 g pro.*

PERFECT PAIR   Nothing goes with clam chowder quite as well as zesty multigrain crackers.

baked cajun seafood and rice

Prep: 40 minutes   Bake: 25 minutes at 350°F   Cook: 15 minutes   Makes 8 servings (1 cup each)

- 1 pound fresh or frozen small shrimp, peeled and deveined
- ¾ cup chopped green sweet pepper
- ½ cup chopped onion
- ½ cup sliced celery
- 2 cloves garlic, minced
- 3 tablespoons butter
- ½ teaspoon dried thyme, crushed
- 3 cups cooked long grain white rice
- 4 strips lower-sodium, less-fat bacon, chopped
- 8 cups torn fresh kale, stems removed
- 2 tablespoons all-purpose flour
- 1½ teaspoons Cajun seasoning
- 2 cups fat-free milk
- 2 cups shredded part-skim mozzarella cheese (8 ounces)
- 12 ounces cooked crabmeat, flaked
- ½ cup shredded Parmesan cheese (2 ounces)
- ½ cup chopped green onions

SIMPLE SWAP

Use fresh spinach or baby Swiss chard for the kale.

1. Thaw shrimp, if frozen; set aside. Preheat oven to 350°F. In a large skillet cook the next four ingredients (through garlic) in 1 tablespoon of the butter over medium heat about 4 minutes or until vegetables are tender. Add thyme; cook and stir 1 minute. Transfer to a bowl. Stir in rice.

2. In the same skillet cook bacon over medium heat until crisp. Add the kale; cook and stir 3 to 5 minutes or until wilted and tender. Remove from heat.

3. In a small saucepan melt the remaining 2 tablespoons butter over medium heat. Stir in flour and Cajun seasoning; cook and stir 1 minute. Stir in milk; cook and stir until thickened and bubbly. Cook and stir 1 minute more. Reduce heat to low. Stir in mozzarella cheese until melted.

4. Lightly grease a 3-quart rectangular baking dish. Spread half of the rice mixture in dish. Layer with half of the kale mixture, half of the shrimp, half of the crabmeat, and half of the cheese sauce. Repeat layers. Sprinkle with Parmesan cheese. Bake, uncovered, 25 to 30 minutes or until bubbly. Sprinkle with green onions.

Per Serving: 380 cal., 13 g fat (7 g sat. fat), 148 mg chol., 653 mg sodium, 31 g carb., 6 g sugars, 3 g fiber, 36 g pro.

black bean and tortellini soup

Start to Finish: 30 minutes   Makes 7 servings (1 cup each)

- 6 ounces uncooked chorizo sausage
- ½ cup chopped onion
- 2 cloves garlic, minced
- 2 cups 50%-less-sodium beef broth or water
- 1 15-ounce can reduced-sodium black beans, rinsed and drained
- 1 14.5-ounce can no-salt-added diced tomatoes, undrained
- 1 8-ounce can no-salt-added tomato sauce
- 1 teaspoon dried oregano, crushed
- ½ teaspoon ground cumin
- 1 9-ounce package refrigerated cheese-filled tortellini
- ¼ cup snipped fresh cilantro
- ¼ cup crumbled queso fresco

1. In a 4-quart Dutch oven cook chorizo, onion, and garlic over medium heat until meat is browned and onion is tender; drain off fat. Stir in the next six ingredients (through cumin). Bring to boililng. Stir in tortellini. Return to boiling; reduce heat. Simmer 8 to 10 minutes or until tortellini are tender, stirring occasionally. Sprinkle with cilantro and queso fresco.

Per Serving: *311 cal., 13 g fat (5 g sat. fat), 38 mg chol., 748 mg sodium, 35 g carb., 6 g sugars, 6 g fiber, 16 g pro.*

PERFECT PAIR   Serve this hearty soup with a salad of shredded jicama, carrots, and kale or cabbage tossed with a lime vinaigrette, snipped fresh cilantro, and pumpkin seeds (pepitas).

portobello-blue cheese pitas with chili aïoli

Prep: 15 minutes   Cook: 5 minutes   Makes 4 servings (1 pita each)

¼ cup light mayonnaise
½ teaspoon chili powder
1 clove garlic, minced
1 tablespoon olive oil
1½ teaspoons white wine vinegar
3 cups mixed baby greens or arugula
4 large portobello mushrooms
2 teaspoons olive oil
¼ teaspoon salt
¼ teaspoon black pepper
4 6-inch Greek pita flatbread rounds,* warmed
¼ cup crumbled blue cheese

SIMPLE SWAP

For a cheese variation, sprinkle with crumbled goat cheese (chèvre) or shredded smoked mozzarella.

1. For aïoli , in a bowl stir together mayonnaise, chili powder, and garlic. In another bowl whisk together the 1 tablespoon olive oil and the vinegar. Add greens; toss to coat.

2. Remove and discard stems from mushrooms. Slice mushroom caps into ½-inch-thick slices. In a large skillet heat the 2 teaspoons olive oil over medium-high heat. Add mushrooms; sprinkle with salt and pepper. Cook about 5 minutes or until tender and golden on edges, stirring occasionally.

3. Spread aïoli on pita bread rounds. Top with greens and mushrooms. Sprinkle evenly with cheese. Fold pita rounds over for sandwiches or eat open-faced.

*TIP: If desired, use pita pockets instead of pita flatbread. Fill pita pocket with aïoli, greens, mushrooms, and blue cheese.

Per Serving: *320 cal., 13 g fat (3 g sat. fat), 9 mg chol., 715 mg sodium, 42 g carb., 5 g sugars, 4 g fiber, 11 g pro.*

spicy mushroom sloppy joes

Start to Finish: 30 minutes   Makes 6 servings (1 sandwich each)

- 1 pound extra-lean (95%) ground beef
- 3 cups sliced fresh cremini mushrooms
- 2 cloves garlic, minced
- ½ cup 50%-less-sodium beef broth
- 1 8-ounce can tomato sauce
- 2 tablespoons Worcestershire sauce
- 2 tablespoons red wine vinegar
- 1 tablespoon molasses
- ½ to ¾ teaspoon ground chipotle chile pepper
- 6 multigrain hamburger buns, toasted
- 6 slices Monterey Jack cheese with jalapeño peppers or cheddar cheese
  Sliced red onion

1. In a large skillet cook the first three ingredients (through garlic) until meat is browned and mushrooms are tender, stirring occasionally. Drain off fat. Stir in the next six ingredients (through chipotle pepper). Bring to boiling; reduce heat. Simmer, uncovered, 5 to 6 minutes or until liquid is reduced. Spoon onto hamburger buns. Top with cheese and sliced onion.

Per Serving: *330 cal., 13 g fat (6 g sat. fat), 66 mg chol., 655 mg sodium, 28 g carb., 9 g sugars, 3 g fiber, 27 g pro.*

PERFECT PAIR   These spicy sandwiches team well with a creamy slaw, such as shredded broccoli slaw mix with thin strips of red sweet pepper and a bottled light coleslaw dressing.

pumpkin-parmesan risotto

Prep: 20 minutes   Cook: 45 minutes   Makes 4 servings (1½ cups each)

- 2 **tablespoons unsalted butter**
- 1 **cup finely chopped onion**
- 1 **clove garlic, minced**
- 2 **cups uncooked Arborio rice**
- ¾ **cup dry white wine**
- 1½ **tablespoons snipped fresh sage**
- 2¼ **to 2½ cups water**
- 1¾ **cups vegetable broth or chicken broth**
- 1 **cup canned pumpkin**
- ½ **cup finely shredded Parmigiano-Reggiano cheese (2 ounces)**
  Parmigiano-Reggiano cheese, shaved (optional)
  Fresh sage leaves (optional)

1. In a 4-quart heavy saucepan melt butter over medium heat. Add onion and garlic; cook about 3 minutes or until tender, stirring occasionally. Add rice; cook and stir 2 minutes. Carefully add wine; cook and stir until liquid is absorbed. Stir in snipped sage.

2. Meanwhile, in a large saucepan bring the water and the broth to boiling; reduce heat to a simmer. Slowly add 1 cup of the broth mixture to rice mixture, stirring constantly. Continue to cook and stir over medium heat until most of the liquid is absorbed. Add another 1 cup of the broth mixture, stirring constantly. Continue to cook and stir until most of the liquid is absorbed. Add enough of the remaining broth mixture, about 1 cup at a time, cooking and stirring just until rice is tender but firm and risotto is creamy.

3. Stir in pumpkin and the shredded cheese. Cook about 1 minute or until heated, stirring occasionally. If desired, top with shaved cheese and sage leaves.

Per Serving: *397 cal., 9 g fat (5 g sat. fat), 25 mg chol., 558 mg sodium, 64 g carb., 5 g sugars, 3 g fiber, 10 g pro.*

PERFECT PAIR   Roasted Brussels sprouts pairs well with this winter risotto. Toss trimmed and halved Brussels sprouts and sliced apples with olive oil, salt, and black pepper. Roast in a 425°F oven about 25 minutes and drizzle with balsamic vinegar.

green-on-green sandwiches

Prep: 45 hours   Chill: 30 minutes   Makes 2 servings (1 sandwich each)

SIMPLE SWAP

Fill whole wheat pita rounds or split sandwich thins instead of bread slices.

- 4   slices whole grain bread
- 2   tablespoons Herb Pesto recipe
- ¼   cup Pickled Red Onions
- ½   cup large spinach leaves
- 1   medium tomatillo or tomato, very thinly sliced
- ¼   of an avocado, thinly sliced and brushed lightly with lime juice
- 1   ounce thinly sliced fresh mozzarella cheese
- ½   cup scored and thinly sliced English cucumber
- 4   leaf or Bibb lettuce leaves

1. Spread bread slices with the Herb Pesto. Arrange Pickled Red Onions over two slices. Layer with the remaining ingredients. Top with the remaining bread slices, pesto sides down. Wrap sandwiches tightly in plastic wrap. Chill at least 30 minutes before serving.

HERB PESTO: In a food processor or blender combine 1½ cups packed fresh basil leaves; ¼ cup toasted slivered almonds; 2 tablespoons each snipped fresh Italian parsley and snipped fresh tarragon; and 1 large clove garlic, quartered. Process until finely chopped. Add 3 tablespoons olive oil, ¼ teaspoon cracked black pepper, and ⅛ teaspoon salt; process to a coarse puree. Transfer pesto to a bowl; press plastic wrap directly onto surface of pesto. Chill. May be made up to 1 week ahead.

PICKLED RED ONIONS: In a bowl combine ½ cup red wine vinegar, 1 tablespoon sugar, and ¼ teaspoon salt, stirring until sugar dissolves. Stir in 1 large red onion, halved and thinly sliced. Cover; let stand at room temperature 1½ hours, stirring occasionally. Chill up to 3 days. Drain before using.

Per Serving: *302 cal., 14 g fat (3 g sat. fat), 10 mg chol., 375 mg sodium, 32 g carb., 7 g sugars, 7 g fiber, 12 g pro.*

broccoli rabe over polenta

Start to Finish: 30 minutes   Makes 4 servings (1 cup each)

- 1 cup quick-cooking polenta mix
- 1 cup chopped sweet onion, such as Vidalia or Walla Walla
- 4 teaspoons olive oil
- 3 cloves garlic, minced
- 1 pound broccoli rabe, coarsely chopped (about 7 cups)
- ½ of a 7-ounce jar (½ cup) roasted red sweet peppers, rinsed, drained, and chopped
- 1 cup vegetable broth or chicken broth
- 1 tablespoon cornstarch
- ¼ cup pine nuts or slivered almonds, toasted

SIMPLE SWAP

Can't find broccoli rabe? Use 3 cups coarsely chopped broccoli florets.

1. Prepare polenta according to package directions. Cover and keep warm.

2. In a large skillet cook onion in hot oil over medium heat 4 to 5 minutes or until tender, stirring occasionally. Add garlic; cook and stir 30 seconds. Add broccoli rabe; cook, covered, about 3 minutes or just until tender. (If using broccoli florets, cook and stir 3 to 4 minutes or until crisp-tender.) Stir in roasted red peppers.

3. In a bowl gradually stir broth into cornstarch; add to vegetable mixture. Cook and stir over medium heat until thickened and bubbly. Cook and stir 2 minutes more. Spoon vegetable mixture over polenta. Sprinkle with nuts.

Per Serving: *394 cal., 11 g fat (1 g sat. fat), 0 mg chol., 256 mg sodium, 67 g carb., 3 g sugars, 11 g fiber, 12 g pro.*

two-bean enchilada casserole

Prep: 25 minutes   Bake: 45 minutes at 350°F   Makes 6 servings (1 cup each)

Nonstick cooking spray
1 tablespoon butter
1 tablespoon all-purpose flour
1 8-ounce can no-salt-added tomato sauce
¾ cup reduced-sodium vegetable broth or chicken broth
1 tablespoon chili powder
1 teaspoon ground cumin
1 teaspoon dried oregano, crushed
⅛ teaspoon ground cinnamon
1 15-ounce can no-salt-added black beans, rinsed and drained
1 15-ounce can no-salt-added pinto beans, rinsed and drained
¾ cup chopped green sweet pepper
1 4-ounce can diced green chile peppers, undrained
½ cup chopped onion
9 6-inch corn tortillas, cut into wedges
2 cups shredded reduced-fat cheddar cheese (8 ounces)
Sliced lettuce, chopped tomato, and/or sliced pitted ripe olives (optional)

SIMPLE SWAP

Get a little more heat with a poblano chile pepper instead of green sweet pepper.

1. Preheat oven to 350°F. Coat a 2-quart rectangular baking dish with cooking spray; set aside. For sauce, in a small saucepan melt butter over medium heat. Stir in flour until smooth. Stir in the next six ingredients (through cinnamon). Cook and stir until thickened and bubbly. Cook and stir 1 minute more. Remove from heat. In a bowl combine the next five ingredients (through onion).

2. To assemble casserole, spread ⅓ cup of the sauce in bottom of the prepared baking dish. Top with three of the tortillas, one-third of the bean mixture, one-third of the remaining sauce, and ⅔ cup of the cheese. Repeat layers. Top with the remaining tortillas, bean mixture, and sauce.

3. Bake, covered, 35 minutes. Sprinkle with the remaining ⅔ cup cheese. Bake, uncovered, about 10 minutes more or until cheese is melted. If desired, top with lettuce, chopped tomato, and/or olives.

Per Serving: 323 cal., 11 g fat (7 g sat. fat), 32 mg chol., 433 mg sodium, 38 g carb., 5 g sugars, 10 g fiber, 19 g pro.

up to
500 calories

THESE RECIPES HAVE A MORE ROBUST CALORIE COUNT BUT CAN STILL BE PART OF YOUR DAILY DIET. YOU'LL FIND COMPLETE MEALS THAT ARE KEY TO HELPING YOU MAINTAIN YOUR IDEAL WEIGHT WHILE EATING WHAT YOU LOVE.

spicy apple crepes with maple cream

Prep: 25 minutes   Chill: 30 minutes   Cook: 10 minutes   Makes 5 servings (2 crepes each)

1   recipe Maple Cream
4   tart cooking apples, such as Granny Smith, peeled, cored, and diced
1   tablespoon lemon juice
½   cup apple juice, apple cider, or water
½   cup raisins or dried cherries
¼   cup sugar
½   teaspoon ground cinnamon
¼   teaspoon ground nutmeg
¼   cup red currant jelly or apple jelly
10 Crepes
    Powdered sugar (optional)

SIMPLE SWAP

Use ½ teaspoon apple pie spice for the cinnamon and nutmeg.

1. Prepare Maple Cream. In a large skillet toss together apples and lemon juice. Stir in the next five ingredients (through nutmeg). Bring to boiling; reduce heat. Simmer, uncovered, about 5 minutes or just until apples are tender, stirring occasionally. Stir in jelly; cook 5 minutes more. Remove from heat; keep warm.

2. Spread half of each crepe with ¼ cup of the apple mixture; fold over. Spoon Maple Cream over filled crepes. If desired, sprinkle crepes with powdered sugar.

MAPLE CREAM: In a blender or food processor combine 1 cup cottage cheese and ½ cup plain low-fat yogurt. Cover and blend 2 minutes or until very smooth. Stir in ½ cup pure maple syrup. Cover and chill at least 30 minutes.

CREPES: In a blender combine 2 eggs, beaten; 1½ cups milk; 1 cup all-purpose flour; 1 tablespoon melted butter; 1 teaspoon sugar; and ¼ teaspoon salt; blend until smooth. Heat a lightly greased small skillet over medium-high heat; remove from heat. Pour in about 2 tablespoons of the batter; lift and tilt skillet to spread batter evenly. Return to heat; cook 1 minute or until browned on one side. Turn crepe over; cook 1 minute more. Slide crepe onto paper towel-lined plate. Repeat with remaining batter, greasing skillet occasionally. If crepes are browning too quickly, reduce heat to medium.

TIP: For a light and easy breakfast option, fill plain crepes with whipped cream cheese spread and sliced strawberries or other fresh berries.

Per Serving: *467 cal., 7 g fat (2 g sat. fat), 59 mg chol., 295 mg sodium, 95 g carb., 69 g sugars, 5 g fiber, 12 g pro.*

huevos tacos con queso

Start to Finish: 25 minutes   Makes 4 servings (2 tacos each)

½ cup chopped red onion
2 teaspoons olive oil
2 cloves garlic, minced
1 15-ounce can no-salt-added pinto beans, rinsed and drained
½ teaspoon ground cumin
¼ teaspoon kosher salt
¼ teaspoon dried oregano, crushed
⅛ teaspoon cayenne pepper
½ cup water
Nonstick cooking spray
10 eggs, lightly beaten
8 6-inch corn tortillas, warmed*
½ cup shredded reduced-fat Mexican four-cheese blend (2 ounces)
½ cup salsa
Fresh cilantro and/or hot pepper sauce (optional)

SIMPLE SWAP

Pinto beans are classic for this type of recipe, but black beans or Great Northern beans work equally well.

1. In a large nonstick skillet cook onion in hot oil about 4 minutes or until softened, stirring occasionally. Add garlic; cook and stir 30 seconds. Remove from heat. Stir in the next five ingredients (through cayenne pepper); mash the beans. Return to heat. Stir in the water, continuing to mash the beans. Simmer, uncovered, until beans thicken and reach spreading consistency (mixture won't be completely smooth). Remove mixture from skillet; keep warm.

2. Rinse and dry skillet. Coat skillet with cooking spray; heat over medium heat. Pour eggs into skillet. Cook, without stirring, until eggs begin to set on bottom and around edges. Lift and fold the partially cooked eggs so the uncooked portion flows underneath. Continue cooking 2 to 3 minutes or until eggs are cooked through but are still glossy and moist. Immediately remove from heat.

3. Spread bean mixture on warm tortillas; top with cooked eggs, cheese, and salsa. If desired, top with cilantro and/or serve with hot pepper sauce. Fold tortillas to eat tacos.

*TIP: To warm tortillas, stack tortillas and wrap in paper towels. Microwave 20 to 40 seconds or until heated. (Or preheat oven to 350°F. Stack tortillas and wrap in foil. Bake about 10 minutes or until heated.)

Per Serving: *402 cal., 19 g fat (6 g sat. fat), 474 mg chol., 605 mg sodium, 31 g carb., 2 g sugars, 6 g fiber, 26 g pro.*

brunch baked apples with greek yogurt

Prep: 30 minutes   Bake: 1 hour at 350°F   Makes 6 servings (1 apple each)

- 6 medium baking apples, such as McIntosh, Rome Beauty, or Granny Smith
- 1 cup orange juice
- 1 cup rolled oats
- ½ cup packed brown sugar
- ⅓ cup slivered almonds, toasted
- 1 tablespoon all-purpose flour
- ¾ teaspoon ground cinnamon
- ¼ teaspoon ground nutmeg
- ⅓ cup butter, melted
- ⅓ cup honey
- 1 6- to 7-ounce carton plain fat-free Greek yogurt or other creamy-style yogurt

SIMPLE SWAP

Drizzle the apples with maple syrup or agave nectar instead of honey.

1. Preheat oven to 350°F. Remove a ½-inch-thick slice from the top of each apple. Using a melon baller, remove core, stopping about ½ inch from the bottom of the apple. Arrange apples in an ungreased 2- to 3-quart rectangular baking dish. (If necessary, remove a thin slice from the bottom of each apple so apples stand upright.) Brush apples with 1 tablespoon of the orange juice.

2. In a bowl combine the next six ingredients (through nutmeg). Stir in melted butter. Fill centers of apples with oat mixture, mounding slightly. Pour the remaining orange juice around apples. Bake, covered, 50 minutes. Bake, uncovered, 10 to 15 minutes more or until apples are tender. Cool slightly. Drizzle apples with honey. Serve with yogurt.

Per Serving: 438 cal., 15 g fat (7 g sat. fat), 27 mg chol., 100 mg sodium, 76 g carb., 57 g sugars, 7 g fiber, 7 g pro.

blueberry-ricotta biscuits

Prep: 25 minutes   Bake: 10 minutes at 375°F   Cool: 5 minutes   Makes 8 servings (1 biscuit each)

- 1   **15-ounce carton ricotta cheese**
- ⅓   **cup honey**
- ½   **teaspoon almond extract**
- 1   **17.3-ounce package (8) refrigerated reduced-fat wheat biscuits**
- ½   **cup blueberry jelly**
- 2   **cups fresh blueberries**
- ½   **cup granola or sliced almonds, toasted**

SIMPLE SWAP

Use strawberry or cherry preserves and strawberries or cherries for the blueberry versions. Or combine the berries.

1. Preheat oven to 375°F. Line two baking sheets with parchment paper. In a bowl stir together the first three ingredients (through almond extract) until smooth.

2. Separate biscuits. On prepared baking sheets, flatten and shape each biscuit into a 5-inch round. Bake rounds 10 to 12 minutes or until golden brown. Remove from oven. Cool 5 minutes.

3. Spread biscuits with jelly and ricotta mixture. Top with fruit and granola. Serve immediately.

Per Serving: *419 cal., 14 g fat (6 g sat. fat), 27 mg chol., 637 mg sodium, 66 g carb., 32 g sugars, 4 g fiber, 11 g pro.*

balsamic onion and steak pasta

Prep: 20 minutes   Cook: 18 minutes   Makes 4 servings (1½ cups each)

- 2 tablespoons olive oil
- 1 pound sweet onions, halved and sliced (about 3½ cups)
- 2 cloves garlic, thinly sliced
- 8 ounces boneless beef sirloin steak, cut into thin bite-size strips
- 2 tablespoons balsamic vinegar
- ¼ teaspoon salt
- ¼ teaspoon black pepper
- 1½ cups dried cavatappi or other short tube pasta
- 1 15- to 19-ounce can cannellini beans, rinsed and drained
- 6 cups torn fresh spinach
- 1 ounce shaved Parmesan cheese

1. In an extra-large skillet heat 1 tablespoon of the oil over medium-low heat. Add onions and garlic. Cook, covered, 13 to 15 minutes or until tender, stirring occasionally. Uncover; cook and stir over medium-high heat 3 to 5 minutes more or until golden. Remove onions from skillet.

2. Add the remaining 1 tablespoon oil to skillet. Add beef; cook and stir 2 to 3 minutes or until browned. Stir in onions, vinegar, salt, and pepper.

3. Cook pasta according to package directions, adding beans the last 2 minutes of cooking. Drain, reserving ½ cup of the cooking water. Return pasta and beans to pan. Add spinach; toss to combine and to wilt spinach. Add beef mixture; toss to combine. Add enough of the reserved pasta water to reach desired consistency. Top with Parmesan and additional pepper.

Per Serving: 426 cal., 12 g fat (3 g sat. fat), 39 mg chol., 596 mg sodium, 50 g carb., 7 g sugars, 9 g fiber, 28 g pro.

PERFECT PAIR   Sauté some thin green beans with chopped walnuts, garlic, salt, and black pepper in olive oil to serve alongside.

southwestern beef kabobs with corn and orzo salad

Prep: 40 minutes   Broil: 8 minutes   Makes 8 servings (1 kabob and 1 cup salad each)

⅔ cup dried orzo

2 cups fresh corn kernels (4 ears)

1 medium orange sweet pepper, cut into bite-size pieces

⅔ cup grape tomatoes, halved

1 14.5- to 15-ounce can kidney beans, rinsed and drained

½ cup thinly sliced red onion

1 small zucchini, halved lengthwise and sliced

1 lime

2 tablespoons olive oil

2 tablespoons honey

3 cloves garlic, minced

1 fresh jalapeño chile pepper, seeded and finely chopped*

2 tablespoons snipped fresh cilantro

½ teaspoon salt

4 teaspoons chili powder

2 teaspoons garlic salt

1 teaspoon ground cumin

1 teaspoon ground oregano

2 pounds boneless beef sirloin, cut into 1-inch cubes

1. If using wooden skewers, soak eight 10-inch skewers in water for 30 minutes.

2. Cook orzo according to package directions, adding corn kernels for the last minute of cooking time. Drain orzo mixture in a colander; rinse with cold water. In a bowl combine orzo mixture and the next five ingredients (through zucchini).

3. Remove 1 teaspoon zest and squeeze ¼ cup juice from lime. In a screw-top jar combine lime zest and juice and the next six ingredients (through salt). Shake well. Add to orzo mixture; mix well.

4. In a resealable plastic bag combine the next four ingredients (through oregano); mix well. Add beef cubes to bag. Seal bag; shake to coat. Thread beef cubes evenly onto skewers.

5. Preheat broiler. Place kabobs on the unheated rack of a broiler pan. Broil 3 to 4 inches from heat 8 to 12 minutes or until desired doneness, turning once. (To grill, grill kabobs, uncovered, over medium heat 8 to 12 minutes or until desired doneness, turning once.) Serve kabobs with orzo salad. If desired, serve with lime slices.

*TIP: Chile peppers contain oils that can irritate your skin and eyes. Wear plastic or rubber gloves when working with them.

TO MAKE AHEAD: Beef can be cubed several hours ahead, wrapped, and refrigerated. Salad can be made and refrigerated up to 24 hours before serving.

Per Serving: *422 cal., 18 g fat (6 g sat. fat), 52 mg chol., 550 mg sodium, 38 g carb., 8 g sugars, 6 g fiber, 30 g pro.*

PERFECT PAIR   Serve with warm whole wheat pita rounds to enjoy the kabobs and salad fajita-style.

asian flank steak roll-ups

Prep: 20 minutes   Marinate: 30 minutes   Grill: 17 minutes   Stand: 10 minutes
Makes 4 servings (1 roll-up each)

12 ounces beef flank steak	1 clove garlic, minced
3 tablespoons orange juice	4 whole wheat flour tortillas
3 tablespoons water	1 medium onion, thickly sliced
2 tablespoons lime juice	2 small red and/or yellow sweet peppers, halved and seeded
1 teaspoon grated fresh ginger	
½ teaspoon dried oregano, crushed	¼ cup hoisin or plum sauce
⅛ teaspoon salt	1 cup shredded napa cabbage
⅛ teaspoon cayenne pepper	

1. Score both sides of steak in a diamond pattern by making shallow diagonal cuts at 1-inch intervals. Place steak in a resealable plastic bag set in a shallow dish. In a bowl combine the next eight ingredients (through garlic); pour over steak. Seal bag; turn to coat steak. Marinate in the refrigerator at least 30 minutes or up to 4 hours, turning bag occasionally.

2. Drain steak, discarding marinade. Grill steak, covered, over medium heat 17 to 21 minutes for medium (160°F), turning once. Remove steak from grill. Let stand 10 minutes. Meanwhile, wrap tortillas in foil. Grill tortilla packet, onion slices, and sweet pepper halves, uncovered, over medium heat 8 to 10 minutes or until tortillas are heated and vegetables are tender, turning packet and vegetables once. Thinly slice steak diagonally across the grain into bite-size pieces. Separate onion into rings and sweet peppers into strips.

3. Spread warm tortillas with hoisin sauce. Top with napa cabbage and steak pieces. Using a slotted spoon, spoon pepper mixture over steak. Roll up tortillas.

Per Serving: *411 cal., 11 g fat (4 g sat. fat), 34 mg chol., 673 mg sodium, 50 g carb., 7 g sugars, 5 g fiber, 26 g pro.*

PERFECT PAIR   Turn these roll-ups into dinner by tossing the steak mixture and cabbage with the hoisin sauce and serving it over hot cooked brown rice instead of in tortillas.

beef stew with butternut squash

Prep: 40 minutes   Cook: 35 minutes   Makes 5 servings (1½ cups each)

- 2 teaspoons olive oil
- 1 pound beef stew meat, cut into 1-inch cubes
- 1 cup chopped onion
- 1 tablespoon grated fresh ginger
- 2 cloves garlic, minced
- 1 pound butternut squash, peeled and cut into 1½-inch cubes (about 2½ cups)
- 1 14.5-ounce can no-salt-added diced tomatoes, undrained
- 1½ cups 50%-less-sodium beef broth
- 1 8-ounce can no-salt-added tomato sauce
- 1½ teaspoons ground cumin
- 1 teaspoon ground cinnamon
- ½ teaspoon crushed red pepper
- 3 cups cooked whole wheat couscous
  Salt (optional)
- ¼ cup sliced almonds, toasted*
- 1 to 2 tablespoons coarsely snipped fresh parsley

SIMPLE SWAP

Save a little time. Look for packaged cubed butternut squash in the produce or freezer section of the supermarket.

1. In a 4-quart Dutch oven heat oil over medium-high heat. Add beef. Cook about 5 minutes or until browned on all sides, stirring to brown evenly. Remove beef. Add onion to Dutch oven. Cook about 6 minutes or until tender but not browned, stirring frequently. Add ginger and garlic. Cook and stir 1 minute more.

2. Return beef to Dutch oven. Stir in the next seven ingredients (through crushed red pepper). Bring to boiling; reduce heat. Simmer, covered, 35 to 40 minutes or until beef is tender. If desired, season with salt. Serve stew in bowls with couscous. Sprinkle with almonds and parsley.

*TIP: Toast almonds in a dry skillet over medium-high heat about 2 minutes or until golden brown, stirring frequently.

TO MAKE AHEAD: Prepare as directed through Step 2, except do not add couscous, almonds, and parsley. Let soup cool. Cover and chill up to 3 days. To reheat, bring stew to boiling. Serve as directed.

Per Serving: *422 cal., 9 g fat (2 g sat. fat), 58 mg chol., 247 mg sodium, 60 g carb., 9 g sugars, 12 g fiber, 30 g pro.*

meatball banh mi

Start to Finish: 35 minutes   Makes 6 servings (1 sandwich each)

- 1 egg, lightly beaten
- ¼ cup fine dry bread crumbs
- 3 tablespoons reduced-sodium soy sauce
- 1 clove garlic, minced
- 1 pound lean ground beef
- 3 medium carrots, cut into thin bite-size strips
- 1 medium onion, thinly sliced
- 2 tablespoons packed brown sugar
- 1 9-ounce package fresh spinach
- 6 whole wheat hoagie buns, split and toasted

1. In a large bowl combine egg, bread crumbs, 1 tablespoon of the soy sauce, and the garlic. Add ground beef; mix well. Shape mixture into about thirty 1¼-inch meatballs.

2. In an extra-large heavy skillet arrange meatballs in a single layer. Cook over medium-high heat 8 to 10 minutes or until browned on all sides. Remove from skillet; cover and keep warm.

3. Add carrots and onion to skillet. Cook and stir 3 to 5 minutes or until tender. Return meatballs to skillet. Add brown sugar and the remaining 2 tablespoons soy sauce. Cook about 2 minutes or until meatballs and vegetables are well coated, stirring occasionally. Add spinach; cook and stir about 3 minutes more or just until wilted. Serve meatball mixture in hoagie buns.

TIP: If you prefer, enjoy these meatballs over hot cooked rice, in pita bread rounds, or on a bed of simple spinach salad.

Per Serving: 417 cal., 11 g fat (4 g sat. fat), 80 mg chol., 829 mg sodium, 55 g carb., 11 g sugars, 4 g fiber, 25 g pro.

PERFECT PAIR   Serve these Vietnamese-style sandwiches with slices of fresh mango drizzled with lime juice.

apple butter pork chops

Start to Finish: 20 minutes   Makes 4 servings (1 pork chop and about 1 cup vegetable mixture each)

- **12 ounces fresh young green beans, trimmed**
- **2 tablespoons water**
- **4 slices peppered bacon, cut into 1-inch pieces**
- **4 pork rib or loin chops, cut ½ inch thick**
- **1 tablespoon soy sauce**
- **⅓ cup apple butter**
- **¼ cup water**
- **1 cup red and/or yellow cherry or grape tomatoes, halved if desired**

1. In a 2-quart microwave-safe casserole or bowl combine green beans and the 2 tablespoons water. Microwave, covered, 4 minutes, stirring once; drain.

2. Meanwhile, in an extra-large skillet cook bacon over medium heat until crisp. Drain bacon on paper towels, reserving 1 tablespoon drippings in skillet.

3. Trim fat from chops. Brush chops with soy sauce. Add chops to the reserved drippings in skillet. Cook over medium-high heat until chops are browned on both sides. Add apple butter and the ¼ cup water to skillet; reduce heat. Cook, covered, 5 minutes. Add green beans, bacon, and tomatoes. Cook, uncovered, 3 to 5 minutes more or until sauce is slightly thickened.

Per Serving: *402 cal., 16 g fat (5 g sat. fat), 80 mg chol., 534 mg sodium, 39 g carb., 28 g sugars, 5 g fiber, 27 g pro.*

PERFECT PAIR   Serve these pan-seared chops and the glazed vegetable mixture over hot cooked barley or brown rice.

spicy pork sandwiches with grilled peach chutney

Prep: 45 minutes   Cook: 5 minutes   Grill: 1 hour   Stand: 15 minutes   Broil: 1 minute
Makes 6 servings (1 sandwich each)

1   1½- to 2-pound boneless pork top loin roast (single loin)
1   tablespoon tandoori seasoning blend
¼   teaspoon salt
6   French rolls or hoagie rolls, split
6   slices Swiss cheese
1   recipe Quick Pickles
1   recipe Grilled Peach Chutney

SIMPLE SWAP

Make your own tandoori seasoning. Combine 1 teaspoon each ground coriander and paprika, ½ teaspoon each garlic powder and ground ginger, ¼ teaspoon salt, and ⅛ teaspoon each ground cardamom and ground turmeric.

1. Sprinkle pork roast with tandoori seasoning blend and salt. Rub in with your fingers. Prepare grill for indirect heat, using a drip pan. Place roast over drip pan. Grill, covered, over indirect medium-low heat 1 to 1½ hours or until done (145°F). Grill French rolls, cut sides down, over direct heat 1 to 2 minutes or until lightly toasted.

2. Remove roast from grill; cover with foil and let stand 15 minutes before slicing. (The temperature will rise 10°F during standing.) Thinly slice roast. Top roll bottoms with pork and cheese. Broil 4 to 5 inches from heat 1 to 2 minutes or until cheese is melted. Top with Quick Pickles, Grilled Peach Chutney, and roll tops.

QUICK PICKLES: Using a vegetable peeler, cut 1 large cucumber into ribbons. In a bowl stir together ¼ cup each sugar, white wine vinegar, and water, and ½ teaspoon kosher salt until salt is dissolved. Add cucumber and ½ cup thinly sliced red onion. Cover and chill until ready to serve, stirring occasionally. Drain before serving.

GRILLED PEACH CHUTNEY: Grill 1 medium peach, halved and pitted, and 1 fresh jalapeño chile pepper, covered, over medium heat 6 to 8 minutes or until lightly charred, turning once. When cool enough to handle, chop the peach. Stem, seed, and chop the jalapeño.* In a medium saucepan combine peach, jalapeño, 2 tablespoons sugar, 2 tablespoons white wine vinegar, 1 teaspoon grated fresh ginger, and ¼ teaspoon kosher salt. Cook and stir over medium heat 5 minutes. Remove from heat; cool. Cover and refrigerate until ready to serve.

*TIP: Chile peppers contain oils that can irritate your skin and eyes. Wear plastic or rubber gloves when working with them.

Per Serving: 446 cal., 14 g fat (7 g sat. fat), 98 mg chol., 771 mg sodium, 40 g carb., 17 g sugars, 2 g fiber, 37 g pro.

skillet pork chops with butter beans, peas, and charred green onions

Prep: 25 minutes   Roast: 10 minutes at 400°F

Makes 4 servings (1 pork chop and ¾ cup vegetable mixture each)

4	pork loin rib chops, cut 1¼ inches thick
1	lemon
2	tablespoons snipped fresh Italian parsley
2	tablespoons snipped fresh tarragon
¼	teaspoon salt
¼	teaspoon black pepper
1	tablespoon olive oil
6	green onions, cut into 2-inch pieces
1	15.5- to 16-ounce can butter beans, rinsed and drained
1	5-ounce package fresh baby spinach
1	cup shelled fresh English peas or frozen peas, thawed
	Lemon wedges

1. Preheat oven to 400°F. Trim fat from chops. Remove 2 teaspoons zest and squeeze 1 tablespoon juice from lemon. In a bowl combine lemon zest and the next four ingredients (through pepper). Sprinkle evenly over chops; rub in with your fingers.

2. In an extra-large oven-going skillet cook chops in hot oil over medium-high heat about 6 minutes or until browned, turning once. Stir green onions into skillet around chops. Transfer skillet to the oven. Roast 10 to 12 minutes or until chops are done (150°F). Remove chops from skillet; keep warm.

3. Stir the lemon juice, beans, spinach, and peas into skillet. Cook and stir until beans are heated through and peas are tender. Serve chops with vegetable mixture and lemon wedges.

Per Serving: 467 cal., 22 g fat (5 g sat. fat), 99 mg chol., 603 mg sodium, 27 g carb., 5 g sugars, 8 g fiber, 43 g pro.

PERFECT PAIR   Add a small baked potato topped with fat-free plain yogurt and snipped fresh chives to each serving.

massaged kale and pork salad

Prep: 20 minutes   Cook: 3 minutes   Makes 4 servings (1½ cups each)

- **6   cups torn fresh kale, stems removed**
- **1   recipe Honey-Grapefruit Vinaigrette**
- **1   15-ounce can cannellini beans, rinsed and drained**
- **1   grapefruit, peeled and sectioned***
- **1   avocado, peeled, seeded, and chopped**
- **½   cup sliced radishes**
- **1   1-pound natural pork tenderloin, trimmed and cut crosswise into ¼-inch-thick slices**
- **¼   teaspoon salt**
- **¼   teaspoon black pepper**
-     **Nonstick cooking spray**

SIMPLE SWAP

Butter beans are a good alternative to cannellini beans.

1. Place kale in a large bowl. Drizzle with Honey-Grapefruit Vinaigrette. Using clean hands, massage kale 3 to 4 minutes or until leaves are lightly wilted and glossy, making sure to massage all the kale evenly. Add the next four ingredients (through radishes); toss to combine.

2. Season pork with salt and pepper. Coat a large nonstick skillet with cooking spray. Heat over medium heat. Add pork and cook 3 to 4 minutes or until no longer pink, turning once. Serve over kale mixture.

HONEY-GRAPEFRUIT VINAIGRETTE: In a screw-top jar combine ¼ cup grapefruit juice, 3 tablespoons honey, 2 tablespoons olive oil, 1 tablespoon snipped fresh mint, and ¼ teaspoon each salt and black pepper. Cover and shake well.

***TIP:** To section grapefruit, use a paring knife to cut off a thin slice from both ends of grapefruit. Place a flat end on a cutting board and cut away the peel and white part of the rind, working from top to bottom. Holding grapefruit over a bowl, cut into center between one section and membrane. Cut along other side of the section next to the membrane to free the section. If desired, use juice in bowl to make Honey-Grapefruit Vinaigrette.

Per Serving: 456 cal., 16 g fat (3 g sat. fat), 74 mg chol., 624 mg sodium, 47 g carb., 21 g sugars, 12 g fiber, 35 g pro.

hot-spiced pork and rice

Prep: 45 minutes   Bake: 1 hour at 375°F   Stand: 10 minutes   Makes 6 servings (2 cups each)

- 1 2- to 2¼-pound boneless pork shoulder roast
- 2 to 3 tablespoons vegetable oil
- 2 cups thinly sliced carrots
- 1 8-ounce can sliced water chestnuts, drained
- 1 cup yellow sweet pepper strips
- ½ cup chopped onion
- 1 cup uncooked long grain rice
- 1 14.5-ounce can reduced-sodium chicken broth
- ½ cup water
- ¼ cup reduced-sodium soy sauce
- 2 tablespoons light-color corn syrup
- 2 tablespoons molasses
- 1 to 2 teaspoons chili paste
- 1 teaspoon Chinese five-spice powder
- ⅓ cup sliced green onions

1. Preheat oven to 375°F. Trim fat from meat. Cut meat into ¾-inch pieces. In an extra-large skillet heat 2 tablespoons of the oil over medium-high heat. Add meat, half at a time, and cook until browned. Transfer all of the meat to an ungreased 3-quart rectangular baking dish. Stir in carrots, water chestnuts, and sweet pepper.

2. If necessary, add the remaining 1 tablespoon oil to skillet. Add onion; cook over medium heat until tender, stirring occasionally. Add rice; cook and stir 1 minute. Stir in the next seven ingredients (through five-spice powder). Bring just to boiling, stirring occasionally. Carefully pour rice mixture over meat mixture in baking dish; stir to combine.

3. Bake, covered, about 1 hour or until meat and rice are tender. Let stand, covered, 10 minutes before serving. Gently stir mixture and sprinkle with green onions.

Per Serving: *432 cal., 11 g fat (3 g. sat. fat), 96 mg chol., 690 mg sodium, 45 g carb., 16 g sugars, 2 g fiber, 36 g pro.*

PERFECT PAIR   Steamed broccoli, snow peas, or green beans cooked until crisp-tender is a colorful accompaniment to this Asian-style dish.

chicken rolls diablo

Prep: 30 minutes   Cook: 30 minutes

Makes 4 servings (1 chicken roll, ¾ cup pasta, and ½ cup sauce each)

SIMPLE SWAP

Turkey breast cutlets can be used for chicken breasts and may not need flattening.

- 2   8-ounce skinless, boneless chicken breast halves
- 1   teaspoon dried Italian seasoning, crushed
- 1   large Swiss chard leaf, stem removed and torn into 4 equal pieces, or 2 ounces fresh spinach
- 8   thin slices prosciutto or deli-sliced ham
- ½   cup shredded part-skim mozzarella cheese
- 1   tablespoon olive oil
- ¼   cup finely chopped onion
- 2   cloves garlic, minced
- 2   14.5-ounce cans no-salt-added fire-roasted diced tomatoes, undrained
- 2   tablespoons red wine vinegar
- ¼   teaspoon salt
- ¼   teaspoon crushed red pepper
- 6   ounces dried angel hair pasta

1. Cut each chicken breast in half horizontally. Using the flat side of a meat mallet, flatten chicken between two pieces of plastic wrap to ¼ inch thick. Sprinkle with Italian seasoning and layer with the next three ingredients (through cheese). Roll up, folding in ends to enclose filling; secure with toothpicks.

2. In a large nonstick skillet cook chicken rolls in hot oil over medium-high heat 4 to 5 minutes or until browned, turning occasionally. Remove rolls from skillet; cover to keep warm.

3. In the same skillet cook onion and garlic in drippings over medium heat 3 to 4 minutes or until tender. Stir in the next four ingredients (through crushed red pepper). Return chicken rolls to skillet. Bring to boiling; reduce heat. Simmer, covered, about 10 minutes or until chicken is no longer pink, turning rolls occasionally. Remove chicken from skillet. Return sauce to boiling; reduce heat. Simmer, uncovered, about 5 to 7 minutes or until sauce is slightly thickened.

4. Meanwhile, prepare pasta according to package directions; drain. Remove toothpicks from chicken; slice rolls. Serve rolls with pasta and sauce.

TO MAKE AHEAD: Prepare rolls as directed through Step 1. Cover with plastic wrap and refrigerate up to 4 hours. Continue as directed.

Per Serving: *453 cal., 12 g fat (3 g sat. fat), 105 mg chol., 857 mg sodium, 39 g carb., 7 g sugars, 5 g fiber, 44 g pro.*

chicken osso buco

Prep: 45 minutes   Slow Cook: 5 hours (low) or 2½ hours (high)
Makes 6 servings (2 drumsticks, ⅔ cup sauce, and ½ cup pasta each)

SIMPLE SWAP

Skinless, boneless chicken thighs make an easy-to-eat substitute for the drumsticks.

- 12 medium chicken drumsticks (about 3 pounds total)
- 2   tablespoons all-purpose flour
- ½   teaspoon salt
- ¼   teaspoon black pepper
- 2   tablespoons olive oil
- 1   cup chopped carrots
- 1   cup chopped celery
- 1   cup chopped onion
- 6   cloves garlic, minced
- 2   tablespoons quick-cooking tapioca
- 1   lemon
- 1   8-ounce can tomato sauce
- ½   cup dry white wine or chicken broth
- ¼   cup chicken broth
- 1   teaspoon dried thyme, crushed
- 3   cups dried penne pasta
     Snipped fresh parsley (optional)

1. Remove and discard skin from chicken. In a resealable plastic bag combine flour, salt, and pepper. Add chicken pieces, a few at time, shaking to coat. In a large skillet cook chicken, half at a time, in hot oil over medium heat about 10 minutes or until golden, turning once. Drain off fat.

2. In a 4- to 5-quart slow cooker combine the next four ingredients (through garlic). Sprinkle with tapioca. Place chicken on vegetables. Remove 1 teaspoon lemon zest and squeeze 1 tablespoon juice from lemon. In a bowl stir together lemon zest, lemon juice, and the next four ingredients (through thyme). Pour over chicken. Cover and cook on low for 5 to 6 hours or on high for 2½ to 3 hours.

3. Before serving, cook pasta according to package directions; drain. Spoon chicken and sauce over pasta. If desired, sprinkle with parsley.

Per Serving: *404 cal., 10 g fat (2 g sat. fat), 118 mg chol., 578 mg sodium, 42 g carb., 5 g sugars, 3 g fiber, 31 g pro.*

oregano chicken with spinach, orzo, and tomatoes

Prep: 20 minutes   Slow Cook: 4 hours (low) or 2 hours (high)
Makes 4 servings (1 chicken breast half and 1 cup pasta mixture each)

- 1 **teaspoon dried oregano, crushed**
- 1 **teaspoon dried basil, crushed**
- 1 **teaspoon dried parsley, crushed**
- ¼ **teaspoon salt**
- ⅛ **teaspoon black pepper**
- 4 **8-ounce skinless, boneless chicken breast halves**
- 1 **tablespoon olive oil**
- 1 **14.5-ounce can reduced-sodium chicken broth**
- 3 **cloves garlic, minced**
- 1 **10-ounce package frozen chopped spinach, thawed and squeezed dry**
- 2 **cups grape tomatoes**
- 1 **lemon**
- 1½ **cups cooked orzo pasta**
- 1 **tablespoon grated Parmesan cheese**
  Snipped fresh oregano

SIMPLE SWAP

For a more economical meal, use 8 skinless, boneless chicken thighs instead of chicken breasts.

1. In a bowl combine the first five ingredients (through pepper). Sprinkle over chicken; rub in with your fingers. In a large skillet cook chicken in hot oil over medium-high heat about 6 minutes or until browned, turning once. Remove from heat.

2. In a 3½- or 4-quart slow cooker combine chicken, broth, and garlic. Add spinach; top with tomatoes. Cover and cook on low for 4 hours or on high for 2 hours.

3. Remove 1 teaspoon zest and squeeze 2 tablespoons juice from lemon. Remove chicken from cooker; cover and keep warm. Using a slotted spoon, transfer spinach and tomatoes to a large bowl; discard cooking liquid. Stir cooked pasta, lemon zest, and lemon juice into spinach mixture. Serve chicken with pasta mixture. Top with Parmesan cheese and snipped fresh oregano.

Per Serving: *414 cal., 10 g fat (2 g sat. fat), 146 mg chol., 595 mg sodium, 24 g carb., 4 g sugars, 3 g fiber, 54 g pro.*

chicken and lentils in apple-curry sauce

Prep: 25 minutes   Cook: 40 minutes   Makes 6 servings (1 thigh, 1½ cups spinach, and ⅔ cup lentils each)

6	skinless, boneless chicken thighs
2	tablespoons olive oil
1	large onion, halved and thinly sliced
4	cloves garlic, minced
1	tablespoon finely shredded fresh ginger
2	tablespoons tomato paste
1	tablespoon mild curry powder
1	teaspoon garam masala
½	teaspoon salt
3	cups reduced-sodium chicken broth
1½	cups lentils, rinsed and drained
3	red and/or green cooking apples, cored and cut into 1-inch pieces
2	5-ounce packages baby spinach (8 to 10 cups)
	Plain yogurt (optional)

SIMPLE SWAP

Use peak-season pears instead of apples. Choose pears that are ripe but still a little firm.

1. In an extra-large skillet with a tight-fitting lid cook chicken thighs in hot olive oil over medium-high heat 4 to 6 minutes or until golden brown, turning once. Transfer chicken to a plate.

2. Add onion to skillet; cook and stir over medium heat 3 minutes. Add garlic and ginger; cook and stir 1 minute more. Stir in the next four ingredients (through salt) until well mixed. Add chicken broth, lentils, and browned chicken thighs to skillet. Bring to boiling; reduce heat. Simmer, covered, 30 minutes.

3. Add apples to skillet. Simmer, covered, about 10 minutes or until lentils are tender. Gradually stir in about 3 cups of the spinach. Divide remaining spinach among serving bowls. Top with chicken thighs, lentil mixture, and, if desired, yogurt.

Per Serving: *436 cal., 10 g fat (2 g sat. fat), 108 mg chol., 658 mg sodium, 49 g carb., 13 g sugars, 19 g fiber, 38 g pro.*

jerk chicken thighs with mango-pineapple relish

Prep: 20 minutes   Slow Cook: 5 hours (low) or 2½ hours (high)   Broil: 3 minutes
Makes 4 servings (2 thighs and about ½ cup relish each)

Nonstick cooking spray
4 pounds bone-in chicken thighs, skinned
⅓ cup reduced-sodium soy sauce
¼ cup molasses
2 tablespoons vegetable oil
1½ tablespoons Jamiacan jerk seasoning
1 3-inch piece fresh ginger, peeled and sliced
1 large jalapeño chile pepper, halved*
4 cloves garlic, peeled and halved
¼ teaspoon cayenne pepper (optional)
¾ cup chopped onion
1 large orange, cut into wedges
1 recipe Mango-Pineapple Relish

1. Lightly coat the inside of a 4- to 5-quart slow cooker with cooking spray. Place chicken in slow cooker; set aside.

2. For sauce, in a food processor or blender combine the next eight ingredients (through cayenne pepper). Cover and process or blend until smooth. Pour ⅔ cup of the sauce over the chicken; toss to coat. Cover and chill the remaining sauce until needed. Add onion and orange wedges to cooker on top of chicken. Cover and cook on low for 5 to 6 hours or on high for 2½ to 3 hours.

3. Lightly coat a broiler pan or baking sheet with cooking spray. Using a slotted spoon, transfer chicken to prepared pan. Brush reserved sauce over chicken. Broil chicken 4 to 5 inches from heat 3 to 4 minutes or until sauce is browned. Serve with Mango-Pineapple Relish.

MANGO-PINEAPPLE RELISH: In a bowl combine 1 cup each finely chopped fresh mango and finely chopped fresh pineapple, ½ cup chopped red cabbage, 2 tablespoons each snipped fresh mint and honey, and ¼ teaspoon salt.

*TIP: Chile peppers contain oils that can irritate your skin and eyes. Wear plastic or rubber gloves when working with them.

Per Serving: *491 cal., 13 g fat (3 g sat. fat), 255 mg chol., 719 mg sodium, 36 g carb., 29 g sugars, 3 g fiber, 56 g pro.*

PERFECT PAIR   Make a bed of hot cooked brown rice or quinoa for this spicy chicken dish. Add steamed broccoli spears for a colorful side.

chicken thighs with gnocchi dumplings

Prep: 15 minutes   Cook: 30 minutes

Makes 4 servings (1 chicken thigh and about 1 cup gnocchi mixture each)

- 4   skinless, boneless chicken thighs (1 to 1¼ pounds)
- ¼   teaspoon black pepper
- ⅛   teaspoon salt
- 2   tablespoons olive oil
- 2   cups quartered fresh mushrooms
- 6   ounces fresh thin green beans
- 1   cup matchstick-cut carrots
- ½   cup chopped onion
- 1   clove garlic, minced
- ½   teaspoon dried thyme, crushed
- 2   tablespoons all-purpose flour
- 2   cups unsalted chicken stock
- 1   16-ounce package shelf-stable whole wheat potato gnocchi
- ¼   teaspoon salt

1. Season chicken with pepper and salt. In an extra-large nonstick skillet cook chicken in 1 tablespoon of the oil over medium heat 13 to 15 minutes or until well browned and chicken is done (170°F), turning occasionally. Transfer chicken to a platter; keep warm.

2. In the same skillet cook the next six ingredients (through thyme) in the remaining 1 tablespoon oil over medium heat about 10 minutes or until tender, stirring occasionally. Sprinkle with flour; cook and stir 1 minute. Stir in stock; bring to boiling, stirring frequently. Stir in gnocchi. Return to boiling; reduce heat. Simmer, uncovered, 3 to 4 minutes or until gnocchi are tender. Season with the ¼ teaspoon salt. Serve gnocchi mixture with chicken.

Per Serving: 435 cal., 13 g fat (2 g sat. fat), 106 mg chol., 822 mg sodium, 49 g carb., 5 g sugars, 6 g fiber, 32 g pro.

PERFECT PAIR   Serve this updated chicken and dumplings with hearty whole grain baguette slices that have been rubbed with garlic, brushed with olive oil, and toasted under the broiler.

curried turkey and couscous pie

Prep: 40 minutes   Bake: 30 minutes at 350°F   Cool: 5 minutes   Makes 6 servings

½   of a 14.1-ounce package (1 crust) rolled refrigerated unbaked piecrust
    Nonstick cooking spray
1   pound turkey breast tenderloins, cut into ½-inch pieces
2   cloves garlic, minced
1½   teaspoons curry powder
⅛   teaspoon salt
⅛   teaspoon cayenne pepper
1   14.5-ounce can chicken broth or vegetable broth
1   cup frozen peas
1   cup uncooked couscous
4   ounces reduced-fat cream cheese (Neufchâtel), softened
¼   cup snipped fresh cilantro
¼   cup mango chutney
½   cup sour cream (optional)
¼   cup toasted sliced almonds (optional)

SIMPLE SWAP

Skinless, boneless chicken breast or trimmed pork tenderloin makes an ideal stand-in for the turkey.

1. Let piecrust stand according to package directions. Meanwhile, preheat oven to 350°F. Coat a large nonstick skillet with cooking spray; heat over medium heat. Add turkey and garlic; cook and stir 1 minute. Sprinkle with curry powder, salt, and cayenne pepper; cook and stir 1 to 2 minutes more or until turkey is no longer pink. Add broth and peas; bring to boiling. Remove from heat; stir in couscous. Cover; let stand about 5 minutes or until broth is absorbed. Stir in cream cheese, cilantro, and chutney.

2. On a lightly floured surface, roll pastry into a 12-inch circle. Press pastry onto the bottom and up the sides of a 9-inch springform pan. Spoon turkey mixture into pastry-lined pan.

3. Bake 30 to 35 minutes or until golden. Cool in pan on a wire rack 5 minutes. Using a small sharp knife, loosen pastry from sides of pan; remove sides of pan. If desired, serve pie with sour cream, almonds, additional chutney, and/or additional cilantro.

Per Serving: *444 cal., 14 g fat (6 g sat. fat), 62 mg chol., 592 mg sodium, 53 g carb., 8 g sugars, 4 g fiber, 27 g pro.*

turkey meatballs with fettuccine

Prep: 45 minutes   Bake: 15 minutes at 400°F   Makes 6 servings (1 cup pasta and 10 meatballs each)

Nonstick cooking spray
1 egg white
1 cup soft whole wheat bread crumbs
½ cup shredded carrot
¼ cup finely chopped onion
¼ cup grated Parmesan cheese
2 tablespoons fat-free milk
2 tablespoons snipped fresh basil
1 teaspoon lemon zest
2 cloves garlic, minced
¼ teaspoon salt
¼ teaspoon black pepper
1 pound uncooked ground turkey breast
8 ounces dried whole wheat fettuccine
8 ounces cremini mushrooms, sliced
1 tablespoon olive oil
2 cups marinara sauce
2 ounces grated or shaved Parmesan cheese

SIMPLE SWAP

Bulk turkey sausage or lean ground beef can stand in for the ground turkey.

1. Preheat oven to 400°F. Line a 15×10-inch baking pan with foil; lightly coat foil with cooking spray. In a large bowl lightly beat egg white. Stir in the next 10 ingredients (through pepper). Add turkey; mix well. Shape mixture into ½-inch meatballs (about 60 meatballs.) Arrange meatballs in a single layer in the prepared pan. Bake about 15 minutes or until no longer pink.

2. Meanwhile, cook fettuccine according to package directions; drain. In an extra-large skillet cook mushrooms in hot oil over medium-high heat until tender, stirring frequently. Reduce heat to medium. Add marinara sauce and cooked meatballs; heat. Serve meatball mixture over fettuccine. Top with shaved Parmesan cheese and additional snipped fresh basil.

TO MAKE AHEAD: Prepare and bake meatballs as directed in Step 1; cool. Place meatballs in an airtight container; cover. Store in the refrigerator up to 24 hours or freeze up to 3 months.

Per Serving: *401 cal., 10 g fat (3 g sat. fat), 49 mg chol., 877 mg sodium, 41 g carb., 9 g sugars, 6 g fiber, 37 g pro.*

lasagna soup

Prep: 20 minutes   Cook: 25 minutes   Makes 6 servings (1¾ cups each)

- 1 pound bulk Italian-flavor turkey sausage or lean ground beef
- ½ cup chopped onion
- ½ cup chopped green sweet pepper
- 3 cloves garlic, minced
- 4 cups reduced-sodium chicken broth
- 1 15-ounce can no-salt-added diced tomatoes, undrained
- 2 8-ounce cans no-salt-added tomato sauce
- 2 teaspoons dried Italian seasoning, crushed
- 10 ounces whole wheat lasagna noodles, broken into bite-size pieces
- ¾ cup part-skim ricotta cheese
- 6 tablespoons finely shredded Parmesan cheese
- 3 tablespoons snipped fresh basil
- ¼ teaspoon crushed red pepper

SIMPLE SWAP

Go vegetarian by using 3 cups sliced fresh mushrooms for the sausage and vegetable broth for the chicken broth.

1. In a large pot cook the first four ingredients (through garlic) over medium-high heat until sausage is browned. Drain off fat. Add the next four ingredients (through Italian seasoning). Bring to boiling; reduce heat. Simmer, covered, 20 minutes.

2. Meanwhile, cook pasta according to package directions; drain. Stir into soup.

3. To serve, spoon ricotta into six bowls. Top with soup. Stir together Parmesan, basil, and red pepper. Sprinkle over soup.

TO MAKE AHEAD: Prepare as directed through Step 1. Let soup cool. Transfer to an airtight container; cover. Store in the refrigerator up to 2 days or freeze up to 3 months. Return soup to a pot and bring to simmering. Continue as directed.

Per Serving: 415 cal., 11 g fat (4 g sat. fat), 64 mg chol., 840 mg sodium, 49 g carb., 9 g sugars, 6 g fiber, 28 g pro.

honey mustard salmon with mango quinoa

Prep: 20 minutes   Grill: 10 minutes

Makes 2 servings (3½ ounces cooked salmon and ⅔ cup quinoa mixture each)

1	8-ounce fresh or frozen skinless salmon fillet
2	teaspoons honey
2	teaspoons spicy brown mustard
1	large clove garlic, minced
1⅓	cups cooked quinoa, room temperature
1	cup chopped fresh or frozen mango, thawed if frozen
2	tablespoons sliced almonds, toasted
1	to 2 tablespoons seeded and finely chopped fresh jalapeño chile pepper*
2	teaspoons olive oil
¼	teaspoon salt
	Pinch black pepper
2	tablespoons snipped fresh cilanto

SIMPLE SWAP

Red quinoa makes a colorful trade for its more traditional cousin.

1. Thaw salmon, if frozen. Rinse fish; pat dry with paper towels. In a bowl stir together honey, mustard, and garlic. Brush both sides of salmon with honey mixture. Grill salmon, covered, over medium heat 4 to 6 minutes per ½-inch thickness of fish or until fish flakes easily, turning once.

2. Meanwhile, in a bowl stir together the next seven ingredients (through black pepper). Top with cilantro. Serve salmon with quinoa.

*TIP: Chile peppers contain oils that can irritate your skin and eyes. Wear plastic or rubber gloves when working with them.

Per Serving: *463 cal., 17 g fat (2 g sat. fat), 62 mg chol., 431 mg sodium, 47 g carb., 19 g sugars, 6 g fiber, 30 g pro.*

spanish cod and orzo packets

Prep: 20 minutes   Bake: 20 minutes at 350°F   Makes 4 servings (1 packet each)

SIMPLE SWAP

Try cod fillets for the tilapia. Bake about 25 minutes for cod.

4 4- to 6-ounce fresh or frozen cod or tilapia fillets
1 cup dried orzo
1 tablespoon snipped fresh oregano
1 cup red and/or yellow cherry or grape tomatoes, halved
¾ cup halved pimiento-stuffed green and/or Kalamata olives
1 small onion, cut into very thin wedges (⅓ cup)
4 cloves garlic, thinly sliced
2 tablespoons olive oil
2 tablespoons lemon juice
¼ teaspoon salt
¼ teaspoon black pepper
1 lemon, thinly sliced

1. Thaw fish, if frozen; set aside. Preheat oven to 350°F. Tear off four 15-inch squares of parchment paper. Cook orzo according to package directions. Stir 1 tablespoon oregano into cooked orzo. Spoon orzo onto one side of each sheet of parchment. Layer the next four ingredients (through garlic) next to orzo. Top with cod fillets.

2. Stir together the next four ingredients (through pepper). Drizzle over fish and vegetables. Top with lemon slices.

3. Fold parchment over fish and vegetables; fold open edges of parchment several times to secure. Place packets in two shallow baking pans. Place pans on separate oven racks. Bake about 20 minutes or until fish flakes easily. Carefully open packets. If desired, sprinkle with additional snipped fresh oregano.

Per Serving: *417 cal., 14 g fat (2 g sat. fat), 71 mg chol., 654 mg sodium, 38 g carb., 4 g sugars, 3 g fiber, 35 g pro.*

wild mushroom ravioli skillet lasagna

Start to Finish: 25 minutes   Makes 4 servings (1½ cups each)

1 egg, lightly beaten
½ of a 15-ounce carton fat-free ricotta cheese
2 tablespoons grated Romano or Parmesan cheese
2 cups lower-sodium tomato pasta sauce with basil
¾ cup water
2 8- to 9-ounce packages refrigerated wild mushroom-filled ravioli or agnolotti
2 cups chopped fresh kale

1. In a bowl combine the first three ingredients (through Romano cheese). In a large skillet combine pasta sauce and the water. Bring to boiling. Stir in ravioli and kale. Return to boiling; reduce heat. Spoon ricotta mixture into large mounds on top of ravioli mixture.

2. Simmer, covered, about 10 minutes or until ricotta mixture is set and ravioli is tender but still firm. If desired, sprinkle with additional grated Romano or Parmesan cheese.

Per Serving: 416 cal., 16 g fat (7 g sat. fat), 118 mg chol., 975 mg sodium, 45 g carb., 9 g sugars, 4 g fiber, 26 g pro.

PERFECT PAIR   Add a crisp green salad of torn romaine, sliced cucumber, slivered red onion, halved cherry tomatoes, and toasted walnuts drizzled with a light balsamic vinaigrette.

white beans and couscous with fresh tomato sauce

Start to Finish: 20 minutes   Makes 4 servings (1¼ cups couscous mixture and ½ cup tomato sauce each)

1¼ **cups boiling water or very hot water**

1 **cup whole wheat couscous**

1 **teaspoon olive oil**

½ **teaspoon salt**

½ **teaspoon black pepper**

1 **15-ounce can no-salt-added cannellini beans (white kidney beans), rinsed and drained**

¼ cup crumbled feta cheese (1 ounce)

2 tablespoons pine nuts, toasted (optional)

2 **tablespoons snipped fresh basil (optional)**

1 **recipe Fresh Tomato Sauce**

SIMPLE SWAP

Substitute finely shredded Parmesan cheese for feta and/or walnuts for the pine nuts.

1. In a bowl or saucepan quickly combine the first five ingredients (through pepper). Cover; let stand 5 minutes. Fluff with a fork. Stir in the next four ingredients (through basil). Serve couscous mixture with Fresh Tomato Sauce.

FRESH TOMATO SAUCE: In a bowl combine 2 cups chopped fresh tomatoes; ½ cup chopped fresh basil; 2 tablespoons olive oil; 2 cloves garlic, minced; and ½ teaspoon each salt and black pepper.

Per Serving: *406 cal., 14 g fat (3 g sat. fat), 8 mg chol., 729 mg sodium, 58 g carb., 6 g sugars, 12 g fiber, 15 g pro.*

spinach-pasta salad with feta and beans

Start to Finish: 25 minutes   Makes 6 servings (2 cups each)

- 1 lemon
- 1 5- to 6-ounce package fresh baby spinach
- 1 15-ounce can Great Northern beans, rinsed and drained
- 1 cup crumbled feta cheese (4 ounces)
- ¼ cup dried tomatoes (not oil-packed), snipped
- ¼ cup chopped green onions
- 2 cloves garlic, minced
- 2 tablespoons olive oil
- 1 tablespoon snipped fresh oregano
- 1 tablespoon snipped fresh lemon thyme or thyme
- ½ teaspoon kosher salt or sea salt
- ½ teaspoon black pepper
- 12 ounces dried cavatappi or farfalle pasta

   Shaved Parmesan or Pecorino Romano cheese

SIMPLE SWAP

Use any short thick pasta in place of the cavatappi.

1. Remove 1 teaspoon zest and squeeze 2 tablespoons juice from the lemon. In a large serving bowl combine lemon zest, lemon juice, and the next 11 ingredients (through pepper); toss to coat. Cover; let stand at room temperature while preparing pasta, stirring occasionally.

2. Cook pasta according to package directions. Drain, reserving ¼ cup of the cooking water. Toss cooked pasta and pasta water with spinach mixture. Serve warm or at room temperature. Top with shaved Parmesan cheese.

TO MAKE AHEAD: Prepare as directed through Step 1. Let stand at room temperature up to 2 hours.

Per Serving: *408 cal., 10 g fat (4 g sat. fat), 19 mg chol., 487 mg sodium, 62 g carb., 3 g sugars, 6 g fiber, 17 g pro.*

CHAPTER 4

savvy
snacks

LOW-CALORIE SNACKS THAT ARE PROPERLY TIMED
THROUGHOUT THE DAY HELP YOU RESIST THE URGE TO
INDULGE IN MINDLESS EATING OR BREAKROOM TREATS.

chocolate-peanut butter granola bars

Prep: 20 minutes   Bake: 10 minutes at 350°F; 12 minutes at 300°F   Makes 18 servings (1 bar each)

Nonstick cooking spray

1	**cup regular rolled oats**
¼	**cup light-color corn syrup**
¼	**cup peanut butter**
3	**tablespoons packed brown sugar**
2	**tablespoons butter**
2	**tablespoons honey**
1	**tablespoon vanilla**
½	**teaspoon salt**
2	**cups crisp rice cereal**
¾	**cup coarsely broken pretzel sticks**
¼	**cup toasted wheat germ**
2	tablespoons chia seeds
¼	**cup miniature semisweet chocolate pieces**

SIMPLE SWAP

Opt for whole flaxseeds instead of chia seeds.

1. Preheat oven to 350°F. Line a 13×9-inch baking pan with foil. Coat foil with cooking spray. Spread oats in a 15×10-inch baking pan. Bake 10 to 15 minutes or until toasted, stirring twice. Remove from oven; let cool. Reduce oven temperature to 300°F.

2. Meanwhile, in a small saucepan combine the next five ingredients (through honey). Heat and stir over medium heat just until peanut butter and brown sugar are melted. Remove from heat. Stir in vanilla and salt. In a bowl stir together the toasted oats and the next four ingredients (through chia seeds). Pour corn syrup mixture over oat mixture; stir to combine.

3. Press oat mixture into the prepared baking dish. Sprinkle chocolate pieces over the top; press pieces firmly into oat mixture. Bake 12 to 15 minutes or until firm. Cool completely in pan on a wire rack.

TO STORE: Layer bars between sheets of waxed paper in an airtight container; cover. Store at room temperature up to 3 days or freeze up to 3 months.

Per Serving: *148 cal., 5 g fat (2 g sat. fat), 3 mg chol., 147 mg sodium, 23 g carb., 11 g sugars, 2 g fiber, 4 g pro.*

198 CALORIES ☐ GLUTEN-FREE ☑ MAKE-AHEAD ☐ HIGH-FIBER ☐ 30-MINUTE ☑ VEGETARIAN

cherry-almond snack mix

Prep: 10 minutes   Bake: 20 minutes at 300°F   Cool: 20 minutes   Makes 10 servings (½ cup each)

- **4** cups sweetened oat square cereal or brown sugar-flavor oat biscuit cereal
- **¾** cup sliced almonds
- **2** tablespoons butter, melted
- **½** teaspoon apple pie spice
- **¼** teaspoon salt
- **1** cup dried cherries and/or golden raisins

1. Preheat oven to 300°F. In a 15×10-inch baking pan combine cereal and almonds. In a bowl stir together butter, apple pie spice, and salt. Drizzle butter mixture over cereal mixture; toss to coat.

2. Bake about 20 minutes or until almonds are toasted, stirring once. Cool in pan on a wire rack 20 minutes. Stir in dried cherries. Cool completely.

TO STORE: Place cooled snack mix in an airtight container; cover. Store at room temperature up to 1 week.

Per Serving: *198 cal., 7 g fat (2 g sat. fat), 6 mg chol., 179 mg sodium, 32 g carb., 15 g sugars, 3 g fiber, 4 g pro.*

SIMPLE SWAP

If you have pumpkin pie spice in your cupboard, use it instead of apple pie spice.

---

189 CALORIES ☑ GLUTEN-FREE ☑ MAKE-AHEAD ☐ HIGH-FIBER ☑ 30-MINUTE ☑ VEGETARIAN

herbed mixed nuts

Prep: 10 minutes   Bake: 15 minutes at 325°F   Makes 12 servings (¼ cup each)

- **1** tablespoon butter, melted
- **1** tablespoon Worcestershire sauce
- **2** teaspoons dried basil and/or oregano, crushed
- **½** teaspoon garlic salt
- **1** cup walnuts
- **1** cup soy nuts
- **1** cup almonds
- **2** tablespoons grated Parmesan cheese

1. Preheat oven to 325°F. Line a 15×10-inch baking pan with foil. In a large bowl combine the first four ingredients (through garlic salt). Add nuts; stir to coat. Spread nuts in the prepared pan. Sprinkle with Parmesan; stir gently to coat evenly. Bake 15 minutes, stirring twice. Cool.

TO STORE: Place cooled nuts in an airtight container; cover. Store at room temperature up to 1 week.

Per Serving: *189 cal., 15 g fat (2 g sat. fat), 3 mg chol., 76 mg sodium, 7 g carb., 2 g sugars, 4 g fiber, 8 g pro.*

SIMPLE SWAP

Use a single nut variety or any combination to equal the 3 cups nuts.

Cherry-Almond Snack Mix

Tropical Smoothies

107 CALORIES   ☑ GLUTEN-FREE ☐ MAKE-AHEAD ☐ HIGH-FIBER ☐ 30-MINUTE ☑ VEGETARIAN

tropical smoothies

Prep: 15 minutes   Freeze: 4 hours   Makes 4 servings (¾ cup each)

- 1 **small banana, peeled and cut up**
- 3 **cups frozen mixed fruit blend (pineapple, strawberries, mango, and/or peaches)**
- 1 **6-ounce carton vanilla fat-free yogurt**
- ¾ **to 1 cup diet tropical blend carrot-base drink, such as V8 Splash brand**

1. Place banana pieces in a resealable freezer bag; freeze about 4 hours or until frozen.

2. In a blender combine frozen banana pieces and frozen fruit blend. Add yogurt and ¾ cup of the tropical drink. Cover and blend until smooth, adding more tropical drink as needed to reach desired consistency. Pour smoothies into glasses.

Per Serving: *107 cal., 0 g fat, 3 mg chol., 33 mg sodium, 25 g carb., 19 g sugars, 2 g fiber, 2 g pro.*

PERFECT PAIR   Add a spear of fresh pineapple or mango to the smoothie when serving it.

112 CALORIES   ☑ GLUTEN-FREE ☑ MAKE-AHEAD ☐ HIGH-FIBER ☐ 30-MINUTE ☑ VEGETARIAN

sweet and spicy apple crisps

Prep: 15 minutes   Bake: 2 hours at 200°F   Makes 4 servings (10 slices each)

- 2 **large apples, such as Braeburn, Jazz, Pink Lady, or Gala, cored**
- ¼ **cup sugar**
- ¼ **teaspoon ground chipotle chile pepper**

SIMPLE SWAP

Vary the spice on the apple crisps by using chili powder, ground ancho chile pepper, or even ground cinnamon.

1. Preheat oven to 200°F. Line two or three baking sheets with parchment paper.

2. Using a mandoline or a serrated knife, cut apples crosswise into ⅛-inch-thick slices. Arrange slices in a single layer on baking sheets. Stir together sugar and chipotle pepper. Sprinkle apple slices with half of the sugar mixture. Use a pastry brush to brush mixture evenly over apple slices. (Or place the sugar mixture in a small sieve. Hold the sieve over apple slices and stir mixture to evenly disperse sugar mixture over apples.) Turn apple slices over; repeat.

3. Bake 2 to 2½ hours or until crisp, turning apple slices and rotating pans every 30 minutes. Cool completely on wire racks.

TO STORE: Place cooled apple crisps in an airtight container; cover. Store at room temperature up to 1 week.

Per Serving: *112 cal., 0 g fat, 0 mg chol., 1 mg sodium, 29 g carb., 25 g sugars, 3 g fiber, 0 g pro.*

berry yogurt parfaits

Prep: 20 minutes   Makes 4 servings (1 parfait each)

- **1   cup plain fat-free Greek yogurt**
- **2   tablespoons honey**
- **1   teaspoon vanilla**
- **½   teaspoon lemon zest**
- **½   cup fresh raspberries**
- **½   cup fresh blackberries, halved if desired**
- **½   cup fresh blueberries**
- **1   cup multigrain oats and honey cereal**
- **Lemon peel strips (optional)**

SIMPLE SWAP

Instead of multigrain cereal, use low-fat granola.

1. Stir together the first four ingredients (through lemon zest). Spoon half of the yogurt mixture into four glasses or parfait dishes. Top with half of the berries and half of the cereal. Repeat layers. Serve immediately or cover and chill up to 30 minutes. If desired, top with lemon peel strips.

TO MAKE AHEAD: The yogurt mixture can be covered and chilled several hours.

Per Serving: *129 cal., 0 g fat, 0 mg chol., 75 mg sodium, 27 g carb., 18 g sugars, 4 g fiber, 6 g pro.*

Crunch-Coated Bananas

110 CALORIES   ☐ GLUTEN-FREE ☐ MAKE-AHEAD ☐ HIGH-FIBER ☑ 30-MINUTE ☑ VEGETARIAN

crunch-coated bananas

Start to Finish: 20 minutes   Makes 4 servings (2 pieces each)

SIMPLE SWAP

Bump up the fiber by using bran cereal flakes instead of cornflakes.

⅓ cup cornflakes, coarsely crushed
2 tablespoons flaked coconut
2 tablespoons vanilla fat-free yogurt
2 tablespoons peanut butter
2 small bananas (each about 5 ounces or about 6 inches long)

1. In a small skillet combine crushed cornflakes and coconut; cook and stir over medium heat 2 to 3 minutes or until coconut starts to brown. Remove from heat. In a bowl stir together yogurt and peanut butter.

2. Slice each banana in half crosswise and then lengthwise to make eight pieces total. Place each piece, cut side up, on a small plate. Spread peanut butter mixture on the banana pieces. Sprinkle evenly with the cornflake mixture.

Per Serving: *110 cal., 5 g fat (1 g sat. fat), 0 mg chol., 62 mg sodium, 16 g carb., 8 g sugars, 2 g fiber, 3 g pro.*

141 CALORIES   ☑ GLUTEN-FREE ☐ MAKE-AHEAD ☐ HIGH-FIBER ☑ 30-MINUTE ☑ VEGETARIAN

carrot cake yogurt

Start to Finish: 15 minutes   Makes 4 servings (⅓ cup each)

1½ cups plain fat-free Greek yogurt
½ cup finely shredded carrot
¼ cup reduced-fat cream cheese (Neufchâtel), softened
1 tablespoon pure maple syrup
½ teaspoon orange zest
¼ to ½ teaspoon ground cinnamon
2 tablespoons chopped walnuts, toasted
2 tablespoons unsweetened shredded coconut, toasted
4 teaspoons pure maple syrup

1. In a bowl beat the first six ingredients (through cinnamon) with a mixer on low to medium until combined. Spoon yogurt mixture into serving dishes. Top with walnuts and coconut and drizzle with maple syrup.

Per Serving: *141 cal., 5 g fat (2 g sat. fat), 5 mg chol., 69 mg sodium, 14 g carb., 12 g sugars, 1 g fiber, 10 g pro.*

PERFECT PAIR   Stir a handful of regular or golden raisins into yogurt mixture.

parmesan dip

Start to Finish: 10 minutes   Makes 8 servings (1½ tablespoons dip and ½ cup vegetables each)

½ cup fat-free sour cream
6 tablespoons finely shredded Parmesan cheese
¼ cup plain fat-free Greek yogurt
2 tablespoons snipped fresh chives
1 tablespoon fat-free milk
1 teaspoon Dijon-style mustard
1 teaspoon snipped fresh dill weed or thyme
¼ teaspoon salt
⅛ teaspoon black pepper
4 cups assorted fresh vegetables, such as radishes, grape tomatoes, green onions, carrot and celery sticks, cucumber slices, sweet pepper strips, and snow pea pods

SIMPLE SWAP

For a quick dipper, use bagged root vegetable chips.

1. In a bowl stir together all of the ingredients except the vegetables. Cover and chill until serving time. Serve dip with vegetables for dipping.

Per Serving: *47 cal., 1 g fat (1 g sat. fat), 4 mg chol., 192 mg sodium, 6 g carb., 2 g sugars, 1 g fiber, 4 g pro.*

italian parmesan pretzels

Prep: 15 minutes   Rise: 20 minutes   Bake: 15 minutes at 400°F   Makes 10 servings (1 pretzel each)

- 1 **pound frozen whole wheat bread dough, thawed**
- 2 **tablespoons grated Parmesan cheese**
- 2 **teaspoons dried Italian seasoning, crushed**
- ¼ **teaspoon garlic powder**
- ¼ **cup light butter with canola oil, melted**

1. Line a baking sheet with parchment paper. Divide dough into 10 equal portions. Roll each portion into a 15-inch-long rope. To shape each pretzel, hold one end of a rope in each hand and form a U shape. Cross the ends over each other and twist. Then lift the ends across to the bottom of the U shape; press to seal. Arrange shaped pretzels on the prepared baking sheet. Cover with waxed paper; let stand in a warm place 20 minutes.

2. Preheat oven to 400°F. Stir together the next three ingredients (through garlic powder). Brush pretzels evenly with half of the melted butter, then sprinkle with the Parmesan mixture.

3. Bake 15 to 18 minutes or until browned. Transfer baking sheet to a wire rack. Drizzle pretzels with the remaining melted butter. Serve warm or cool completely on baking sheet on a wire rack.

TO STORE: Layer cooled pretzels between sheets of waxed paper in an airtight container; cover. Store at room temperature up to 3 days.

Per Serving: *141 cal., 4 g fat (1 g sat. fat), 3 mg chol., 303 mg sodium, 22 g carb., 0 g sugars, 2 g fiber, 6 g pro.*

PERFECT PAIR   Serve these Italian-style pretzels with individual bowls of warm marinara sauce for dipping.

88 CALORIES   ☑ GLUTEN-FREE ☐ MAKE-AHEAD ☐ HIGH-FIBER ☑ 30-MINUTE ☑ VEGETARIAN

pb and jelly poppers

Start to Finish: 15 minutes   Makes 4 servings (3 poppers each)

- ⅓ cup light cream cheese spread
- 1 tablespoon powdered peanut butter
- ¼ teaspoon ground ginger or apple pie spice
- 12 miniature caramel corn- or apple-cinnamon-flavor rice cakes
- ¼ cup desired-flavor sugar-free preserves
- 2 tablespoons miniature semisweet chocolate pieces (optional)

1. Stir together cream cheese, peanut butter, and ginger. Spread on rice cakes and top with preserves. If desired, sprinkle with chocolate pieces.

Per Serving: 88 cal., 4 g fat (2 g sat. fat), 13 mg chol., 170 mg sodium, 13 g carb., 3 g sugars, 0 g fiber, 2 g pro.

PERFECT PAIR   Enjoy these poppers with a glass of cold fat-free milk.

87 CALORIES   ☑ GLUTEN-FREE ☑ MAKE-AHEAD ☐ HIGH-FIBER ☐ 30-MINUTE ☑ VEGETARIAN

choco-cereal-nut clusters

Prep: 35 minutes   Chill: 1 hour   Makes 36 servings (1 cluster each)

- 1 10-ounce package dark chocolate pieces or 1⅔ cups semisweet chocolate pieces
- 1 tablespoon shortening
- 3½ cups bite-size rice-and-corn cereal, such as Crispix brand, or bite-size corn square cereal
- 1 cup unsalted dry-roasted almonds, coarsely chopped
- ⅔ cup dried cranberries

SIMPLE SWAP

Instead of cranberries, you can use snipped dried cherries, dried blueberries, or golden raisins.

1. Line two large baking sheets with waxed paper. Microwave chocolate pieces and shortening 1½ to 2 minutes or until melted and smooth, stirring every 30 seconds. Add cereal, almonds, and cranberries; stir to completely coat with chocolate mixture.

2. Using a 1- to 2-tablespoon cookie scoop,* pack mixture into scoop; drop onto the prepared baking sheets. Chill about 1 hour or until set.

*TIP: If you do not have a cookie scoop, use two tablespoons and lightly pack the mixture between the spoons before dropping onto prepared baking sheets.

TO STORE: Layer clusters between sheets of waxed paper in an airtight container; cover. Store in the refrigerator up to 1 week or freeze up to 1 month.

Per Serving: 87 cal., 5 g fat (2 g sat. fat), 1 mg chol., 23 mg sodium, 10 g carb., 6 g sugars, 1 g fiber, 1 g pro.

PB and Jelly Poppers

blueberry oat-chia seed muffins

Prep: 20 minutes   Bake: 10 minutes at 350°F   Cool: 5 minutes   Makes 18 servings (2 muffins each)

Nonstick cooking spray
1¼ cups all-purpose flour
¾ cup regular rolled oats
⅓ cup sugar
2 tablespoons chia seeds, ground
2 teaspoons baking powder
¼ teaspoon salt
1 egg, beaten
¾ cup fat-free milk
¼ cup vegetable oil
¾ cup fresh blueberries
Powdered sugar (optional)

SIMPLE SWAP

Substitute a chopped banana for the blueberries.

1. Preheat oven to 350°F. Lightly coat thirty-six 1¾-inch muffin cups with cooking spray or line with mini paper bake cups. In a bowl combine the next six ingredients (through salt). Make a well in the center of flour mixture.

2. In another bowl combine egg, milk, and oil. Add egg mixture all at once to flour mixture. Stir just until moistened (batter should be lumpy). Fold in blueberries.

3. Spoon a scant tablespoon batter into each prepared muffin cup, filling each two-thirds full. Bake about 10 minutes or until a toothpick inserted in centers comes out clean. Cool in muffin cups on a wire rack 5 minutes. Remove from muffin cups. Serve warm or at room temperature. If desired, dust muffins with powdered sugar. Serve within 1 day of baking.

Per Serving: *108 cal., 4 g fat (1 g sat. fat), 11 mg chol., 95 mg sodium, 15 g carb., 5 g sugars, 1 g fiber, 2 g pro.*

CHAPTER 5

smart desserts

DESSERTS ARE NOT OFF THE TABLE WHEN YOU ARE COUNTING CALORIES. SATISFY YOUR SWEET TOOTH WITH HIGH-QUALITY TREATS IN SENSIBLE PORTIONS.

berry tart with lemon cookie crust

Prep: 30 minutes   Bake: 12 minutes at 375°F   Makes 8 servings (1 wedge each)

- ¼ cup butter, softened
- ¼ cup granulated sugar
- 1 teaspoon lemon zest
- ½ teaspoon baking powder
- ½ teaspoon vanilla
- ⅛ teaspoon salt
- 1 egg, lightly beaten, or 2 tablespoons refrigerated or frozen egg product, thawed
- 1¼ cups all-purpose flour
- ¾ cup tub-style fat-free cream cheese, softened
- 2 tablespoons powdered sugar
- 1 teaspoon lemon zest
- ½ cup plain fat-free Greek yogurt
- 2 cups fresh blueberries, blackberries, and/or raspberries

  Frozen light whipped dessert topping, thawed, and/or fresh mint sprigs (optional)

SIMPLE SWAP

Slice fresh strawberries to scatter over the tart instead of mixed whole berries.

1. Preheat oven to 375°F. For crust, in a bowl beat butter with a mixer on medium 30 seconds. Add the next five ingredients (through salt); beat until combined. Beat in egg. Beat in flour. If necessary, knead gently until combined.

2. Press dough onto bottom and up sides of a 9-inch round tart pan with removable bottom. Line crust with a double thickness of foil. Bake crust 6 minutes. Remove foil; bake 6 to 7 minutes more or until crust is lightly browned. Cool on wire rack.

3. Meanwhile, for lemon cream, in a bowl stir together the next three ingredients (through lemon zest). Fold in yogurt. Spread in bottom of cooled crust. Top with berries. If desired, garnish with whipped topping and/or fresh mint. Remove sides of pan; cut into wedges.

INDIVIDUAL BERRY TARTS: Prepare crust as directed, except divide dough into eight equal portions. Press each portion onto bottoms and up sides of eight 3½-inch tart pans with removable bottoms. Bake as directed, except after removing foil, reduce baking time to 4 to 6 minutes. Continue as directed. Makes 8 tarts.

Per Serving: *217 cal., 7 g fat (4 g sat. fat), 41 mg chol., 291 mg sodium, 31 g carb., 14 g sugars, 1 g fiber, 8 g pro.*

silky chocolate pie

Prep: 25 minutes   Chill: 24 hours   Cool: 15 minutes   Chill: 3 hours
Makes 10 servings (1 wedge each)

- 5   cups plain low-fat or fat-free yogurt* or 2 cups plain fat-free Greek yogurt**
- 1   envelope unflavored gelatin
- ½   cup fat-free milk
- ½   of an 8-ounce package reduced-fat cream cheese (Neufchâtel), softened
- 4   ounces semisweet chocolate, chopped
- ½   cup sugar
- ½   teaspoon vanilla
- 1   purchased reduced-fat graham cracker crumb pie shell
- ¾   cup frozen light whipped dessert topping, thawed, and/or chocolate curls (optional)

SIMPLE SWAP

For chocolate lovers, substitute a chocolate crumb piecrust for the graham cracker crust.

1. For yogurt cheese, line a yogurt strainer, sieve, or a small colander with three layers of 100-percent-cotton cheesecloth or a clean paper coffee filter. Suspend lined strainer over a bowl. Spoon yogurt into strainer; cover with plastic wrap. Chill 24 hours. Discard liquid. You should have 2 to 2½ cups yogurt cheese.

2. In a small saucepan sprinkle gelatin over milk; let stand 5 minutes. Heat and stir milk mixture over low heat just until gelatin is dissolved. Gradually whisk in cream cheese until melted. Add chocolate; heat and stir over low heat until chocolate is melted. Remove from heat. Stir in sugar and vanilla. Transfer mixture to a bowl; cool 15 minutes.

3. Stir about one-fourth of the yogurt cheese into chocolate mixture until smooth. Fold in the remaining yogurt cheese. Spread filling evenly in the pie shell. Cover pie loosely; chill 3 to 24 hours. Cut into wedges. If desired, top with dessert topping and/or chocolate curls.

*TIP: Be sure to use a brand of yogurt that contains no gums, gelatin, or fillers. These ingredients may prevent the whey from separating from the curd when making the yogurt cheese.

**TIP: If you use Greek yogurt, omit Step 1.

Per Serving: *235 cal., 9 g fat (4 g sat. fat), 9 mg chol., 140 mg sodium, 31 g carb., 23 g sugars, 1 g fiber, 7 g pro.*

snickerdoodle custard pie

Prep: 30 minutes   Bake: 12 minutes at 450°F; 55 minutes at 350°F   Cool: 2 hours
Makes 12 servings (1 wedge each)

½ of a 15-ounce package rolled refrigerated unbaked piecrust (1 crust)	⅛ teaspoon salt
1 ounce bittersweet chocolate, melted	⅛ teaspoon ground nutmeg
1 cup refrigerated or frozen egg product, thawed, or 4 eggs	2 cups fat-free half-and-half
⅓ cup sugar	1 teaspoon sugar
2 teaspoons vanilla	½ teaspoon unsweetened cocoa powder
¼ teaspoon ground cinnamon	⅛ teaspoon ground cinnamon
	⅛ teaspoon ground nutmeg
	1 ounce bittersweet chocolate, melted

1. Preheat oven to 450°F. Let crust stand according to package directions. Unroll crust; place in a 9-inch pie plate. Fold under extra crust even with edge of plate; flute edge. Prick bottom and sides of crust with a fork. Line crust with a double thickness of foil.

2. Bake 8 minutes; remove foil. Bake 4 to 6 minutes more or until crust is lightly browned. Cool on a wire rack. Reduce oven temperature to 350°F. Spread or brush 1 ounce melted chocolate over the bottom and sides of the cooled crust. Let stand until chocolate is set.

3. For filling, in a bowl lightly beat eggs with a fork. Stir in the next five ingredients (through nutmeg). Gradually whisk in half-and-half until well combined. Place the baked crust on oven rack. Carefully pour filling into the crust (crust will be full). To prevent overbrowning, cover edge of pie with foil.

4. Bake 55 to 60 minutes or until a 1-inch area around outside edge is puffed and set (center will still be jiggly and appear undone). Remove foil. Cool completely on a wire rack (pie will set upon cooling). Cover and chill within 2 hours.

5. Before serving, stir together the next four ingredients (through nutmeg). Sprinkle spice mixture over pie. Cut pie into wedges. Drizzle with the remaining melted chocolate.*

*TIP: To drizzle melted chocolate, place it in a resealable plastic bag; seal bag. Snip off corner of bag and squeeze to drizzle chocolate over individual wedges.

TO MAKE AHEAD: Cover and chill pie up to 24 hours.

Per Serving: 149 cal., 6 g fat (3 g sat. fat), 4 mg chol., 191 mg sodium, 21 g carb., 10 g sugars, 0 g fiber, 4 g pro.

PERFECT PAIR   Enjoy this pie with a cup of hot coffee or tea.

pear-pecan crisp

Prep: 20 minutes   Bake: 35 minutes at 375°F   Cool: 20 minutes   Makes 8 servings (¾ cup each)

SIMPLE SWAP

Substitute apples for the pears. Increase the initial bake time in Step 1 to 20 minutes.

- 6 medium pears*
- ¼ cup pure maple syrup
- 2 tablespoons white whole wheat flour
- ¼ teaspoon ground nutmeg
- ¼ teaspoon ground cardamom
- ⅛ teaspoon salt
- ½ cup chopped pecans
- ⅓ cup rolled oats
- 2 tablespoons butter, melted
- 2 tablespoons pure maple syrup
- ¼ teaspoon ground cinnamon
- 2 cups low-fat vanilla ice cream or frozen yogurt (optional)

1. Preheat oven to 375°F. Quarter, core, and thinly slice the pears. In a bowl toss together pears and the ¼ cup maple syrup. Sprinkle with the next four ingredients (through salt); toss to combine. Transfer pear mixture to a 2-quart rectangular baking dish. Cover with foil; bake 10 minutes.

2. Stir together the next five ingredients (through cinnamon). Uncover pears; spoon pecan mixture over pears. Bake, uncovered, 25 to 30 minutes or until filling is bubbly and topping is lightly browned. Cool in dish on a wire rack about 20 minutes. If desired, serve warm with ice cream.

*TIP: The pears should be just ripe for best results.

Per Serving: *201 cal., 8 g fat (2 g sat. fat), 8 mg chol., 65 mg sodium, 34 g carb., 23 g sugars, 5 g fiber, 2 g pro.*

chocolate ravioli

Prep: 20 minutes   Bake: 12 minutes at 375°F   Makes 10 servings (2 ravioli each)

Nonstick cooking spray
½ cup light cream cheese spread
2 tablespoons sugar
2 ounces milk chocolate, finely chopped (⅓ cup)
20 wonton wrappers
1 egg
1 tablespoon water
2 tablespoons sugar-free caramel-flavor ice cream topping
1 tablespoon sliced almonds or chopped pecans, toasted

SIMPLE SWAP

Chop up some dark chocolate instead of milk chocolate if you want these a little less sweet.

1. Preheat oven to 375°F. Line a large baking sheet with foil. Coat foil with cooking spray. For filling, stir together the cream cheese and sugar until smooth. Stir in the chopped chocolate.

2. Lay wonton wrappers on a work surface. Spoon 1½ teaspoons filling into the center of each wrapper. Lightly moisten edges of wrappers with water. To form triangles, fold two opposite corners together, pressing edges to seal. If desired, use a fluted pastry wheel to trim edges of triangles. Whisk together egg and the water. Brush egg mixture over filled ravioli.

3. Place ravioli on prepared baking sheet. Bake 12 to 14 minutes or until golden brown and crisp. Place ravioli on plates. Drizzle with ice cream topping and sprinkle with almonds. Serve warm.

Per Serving: *134 cal., 5 g fat (3 g sat. fat), 29 mg chol., 165 mg sodium, 19 g carb., 7 g sugars, 0 g fiber, 3 g pro.*

pumpkin cupcakes with cream cheese frosting

Prep: 30 minutes   Bake: 18 minutes at 350°F   Makes 12 servings (1 cupcake each)

- ¾ **cup all-purpose flour**
- ¼ **cup flaxseed meal**
- 1 **teaspoon baking powder**
- 1 **teaspoon pumpkin pie spice**
- ½ **teaspoon baking soda**
- ¼ **teaspoon salt**
- 2 **eggs**
- ¾ **cup canned pumpkin**
- ⅔ **cup agave nectar**
- ¼ **cup canola oil**
- 1 **recipe Cream Cheese Frosting**
  Freshly grated nutmeg (optional)

SIMPLE SWAP

Instead of frosting cupcakes, dust them with powdered sugar.

1. Preheat oven to 350°F. Grease and lightly flour twelve 2½-inch muffin cups. Or line cups with paper baking cups and lightly coat cups with nonstick cooking spray.

2. In a bowl stir together the first six ingredients (through salt). In another bowl lightly whisk eggs. Whisk in the next three ingredients (through oil). Add pumpkin mixture all at once to flour mixture. Stir just until combined. Spoon batter evenly into prepared muffin cups.

3. Bake 18 to 20 minutes or until a toothpick inserted in centers comes out clean. Cool in pan on a wire rack 5 minutes. Remove cupcakes from pan; cool completely on wire rack.

4. Spread Cream Cheese Frosting on cooled cupcakes. If desired, sprinkle with nutmeg. Serve immediately or store cupcakes in an airtight container in the refrigerator. Serve the same day they are made.

CREAM CHEESE FROSTING: In a bowl combine 4 ounces reduced-fat cream cheese (Neufchâtel), softened; 2 tablespoons agave nectar; 1 to 2 tablespoons butter, softened; and ½ teaspoon vanilla.

Per Serving: *196 cal., 9 g fat (3 g sat. fat), 41 mg chol., 194 mg sodium, 26 g carb., 17 g sugars, 2 g fiber, 3 g pro.*

raspberry sorbet

Prep: 20 minutes   Chill: 1 hour   Freeze: 10 hours   Stand: 5 minutes   Makes 9 servings (⅓ cup each)

- **1 cup sugar**
- **1 cup water**
- **2 tablespoons lemon juice**
- **3 cups fresh raspberries**
- **2 tablespoons orange juice**

1. For syrup, in a medium saucepan heat and stir sugar and the water over medium heat just until simmering and sugar is dissolved. Remove from heat; stir in lemon juice. Transfer to a bowl; cover and chill completely.

2. Place raspberries and orange juice in a food processor or blender. Cover and process until smooth. Press puree through a fine-mesh sieve; discard seeds. Stir puree into chilled syrup.

3. Spread raspberry mixture in a 2-quart square baking dish. Cover and freeze about 4 hours or until firm. Break up mixture with a fork; place in food processor or blender, half at a time if necessary. Cover and process 30 to 60 seconds or until smooth and lightened in color. Return sorbet to dish; cover and freeze 6 to 8 hours more or until firm. Let stand at room temperature 5 minutes before serving.

Per Serving: *110 cal., 0 g fat, 0 mg chol., 1 mg sodium, 28 g carb., 25 g sugars, 3 g fiber, 1 g pro.*

MANGO SORBET: Prepare as directed, except substitute 3 cups cut-up, peeled mango for the raspberries. Omit pressing fruit through sieve. Makes 4 cups.

Per Serving: *94 cal., 0 g fat, 0 mg chol., 1 mg sodium, 24 g carb., 25 g sugars, 1 g fiber, 0 g pro.*

PERFECT PAIR   Top sorbet with additional fresh raspberries and/or dark chocolate curls.

almond-lemon gelato

Prep: 30 minutes   Chill: 2 hours   Freeze: according to manufacturer's directions
Makes 16 servings (½ cup each)

12	**egg yolks, lightly beaten**
4	**cups whole milk**
1⅓	**cups sugar**
1	**lemon**
½	**cup frozen lemonade concentrate**
⅓	cup chopped toasted almonds

SIMPLE SWAP

Pistachio nuts are a colorful alternative to almonds.

1. In a large saucepan combine the first three ingredients (through sugar). Using a vegetable peeler, cut long strips of peel from the lemon. Add lemon peel to milk mixture. Cook over medium heat, stirring constantly with a wooden spoon or a heatproof rubber spatula, until mixture thickens and just coats the back of a spoon.

2. Immediately place saucepan in a large bowl of ice water; stir constantly 3 to 4 minutes or until mixture is cool. Remove and discard lemon peel. Transfer milk mixture to a bowl. Cover and chill about 2 hours or until well chilled.

3. Stir lemonade concentrate and almonds into milk mixture. In a 4- to 5-quart ice cream freezer freeze mixture according to manufacturer's directions. If desired, transfer gelato to a covered freezer container and ripen in the freezer about 4 hours before serving. If desired, top with additional chopped almonds.

Per Serving: *174 cal., 7 g fat (2 g sat. fat), 144 mg chol., 33 mg sodium, 25 g carb., 24 g sugars, 0 g fiber, 4 g pro.*

molten chocolate cakes with coconut cream

Prep: 30 minutes   Bake: 12 minutes at 350°F   Stand: 5 minutes
Makes 6 servings (1 cake and 2 tablespoons coconut cream each)

⅓ cup refrigerated original coconut milk
¾ teaspoon unflavored gelatin
3 tablespoons granulated sugar
¼ teaspoon clear vanilla
⅛ teaspoon coconut extract (optional)
½ cup all-purpose flour
3 tablespoons unsweetened cocoa powder
¼ teaspoon baking soda
⅛ teaspoon salt
2 egg whites

¼ cup packed brown sugar
2 tablespoons fat-free milk
2 tablespoons canola oil
½ teaspoon vanilla
¼ cup dark chocolate pieces or chopped dark chocolate
3 tablespoons fat-free half-and-half
2 tablespoons shredded coconut, lightly toasted

1. For coconut cream, pour coconut milk into a medium stainless-steel bowl. Sprinkle gelatin over milk. Let stand 5 minutes. Place the bowl in a large saucepan or Dutch oven with about 3 inches of simmering water in the bottom. Heat over medium heat 2 to 3 minutes or until gelatin is dissolved, stirring frequently (the milk may look separated).

2. Remove bowl from saucepan; place bowl in a large bowl half-filled with ice. Add 1 tablespoon of the granulated sugar, the clear vanilla, and, if desired, coconut extract to milk mixture. Beat with a mixer on high about 8 minutes or until thickened and stiff peaks form (tips stand straight).

3. For cakes, preheat oven to 350°F. Grease six 2½-inch muffin cups. In a bowl whisk together the next four ingredients (through salt). In another bowl whisk together the remaining 2 tablespoons granulated sugar and the next five ingredients (through vanilla). Add all at once to flour mixture. Whisk until well combined. Spoon evenly into prepared muffin cups. Bake about 9 minutes or until puffed, edges are firm, and centers look like batter.

4. Meanwhile, in a bowl combine chocolate pieces and half-and-half. Microwave, uncovered, on 30% power (medium-low) 1 to 1½ minutes or until chocolate is nearly melted, stirring once. Let stand 2 minutes. Stir until smooth.

5. Remove cakes from oven. Use two forks to open centers of cakes slightly. Spoon melted chocolate into centers of cakes. Bake 3 minutes more. Let stand in pan on a wire rack 5 minutes. Loosen cakes from edges of cups. Use two spoons to lift cakes out of cups. Invert cakes onto plates. Spoon the coconut cream on top and sprinkle with toasted coconut. Serve immediately.

Per Serving: *219 cal., 9 g fat (3 g sat. fat), 0 mg chol., 143 mg sodium, 33 g carb., 22 g sugars, 2 g fiber, 5 g pro.*

PERFECT PAIR   Serve warm cakes with a small spoonful of fat-free frozen vanilla yogurt.

blueberry-lemon shortcakes

Prep: 25 minutes   Bake: 8 minutes at 400°F   Makes 8 servings (1 shortcake each)

- 1 cup all-purpose flour
- ¼ cup quick-cooking rolled oats
- 1½ teaspoons baking powder
- ¼ teaspoon baking soda
- ⅛ teaspoon salt
- 3 tablespoons cold butter, cut up
- 1 egg
- 3 tablespoons fat-free milk
- 3 tablespoons honey
- 2 tablespoons plain fat-free Greek yogurt
- 2 teaspoons lemon zest
- 1 recipe Honey-Yogurt Cream
- 1 cup fresh blueberries

SIMPLE SWAP

Any fresh berries or cut-up fruit can stand in for blueberries in these shortcakes.

1. Preheat oven to 400°F. In a bowl stir together the first five ingredients (through salt). Using a pastry blender, cut in butter until mixture resembles coarse crumbs. Make a well in the center of mixture.

2. In another bowl beat egg lightly with a fork. Stir in milk, 2 tablespoons of the honey, the yogurt, and lemon zest. Add egg mixture all at once to flour mixture. Stir just until moistened.

3. Using a large spoon, drop dough into eight mounds onto a lightly greased baking sheet. Bake 8 to 10 minutes or until golden. Remove shortcakes from baking sheet; cool on a wire rack.

4. Split shortcakes in half horizontally. Top bottom halves with Honey-Yogurt Cream and blueberries. Add shortcake tops and drizzle with the remaining 1 tablespoon honey. Serve immediately.

HONEY-YOGURT CREAM: Stir together one 6-ounce carton plain fat-free Greek yogurt and 1 tablespoon honey. Fold in ½ cup whipped cream.

TO MAKE AHEAD: Prepare as directed through Step 3. Place cooled shortcakes in an airtight container; cover. Store at room temperature up to 2 days.

Per Serving: 199 cal., 8 g fat (5 g sat. fat), 45 mg chol., 230 mg sodium, 27 g carb., 12 g sugars, 1 g fiber, 6 g pro.

creamy rice pudding

Prep: 20 minutes   Cook: 25 minutes   Makes 6 servings (½ cup each)

1 **cup water**
¾ **cup milk**
¼ **teaspoon salt**
½ **cup Arborio or long grain rice**
1 **teaspoon butter**
1 **cup half-and-half**
½ **of a vanilla bean, halved lengthwise**
2 **egg yolks**
⅓ **cup sugar**

SIMPLE SWAP

Substitute
1 teaspoon vanilla
extract for the
vanilla bean;
stir into sauce
after thickening
in Step 2.

1. In a medium saucepan heat the first three ingredients (through salt) over medium heat until nearly boiling. Stir in rice and butter. Bring to boiling; reduce heat. Simmer, covered, over very low heat 25 to 30 minutes or until thick and nearly all liquid is absorbed, stirring every 5 minutes. Transfer to a bowl.

2. Meanwhile, place half-and-half in a small saucepan. Using a paring knife, scrape seeds from inside of vanilla bean; add seeds to pan. Heat just to boiling. In a bowl whisk together yolks and sugar. Gradually whisk in hot half-and-half; return all to saucepan. Cook and stir over medium-low heat 3 to 5 minutes or until sauce thickens and coats the back of a spoon.

3. Stir sauce into rice; serve warm. Or cover and chill several hours or overnight. If desired, just before serving, stir in additional half-and-half until desired consistency.

Per Serving: *189 cal., 7 g fat (4 g sat. fat), 89 mg chol., 134 mg sodium, 27 g carb., 13 g sugars, 0 g fiber, 4 g pro.*

fruited oatmeal cookies

Prep: 25 minutes   Bake: 19 minutes at 375°F   Makes 48 servings (1 cookie each)

 2 cups rolled oats
    Nonstick cooking spray
 ½ cup butter, softened
1½ cups packed brown sugar
 ¾ teaspoon baking soda
 ¼ teaspoon salt
 ¼ teaspoon ground allspice
 1 6-ounce carton plain low-fat yogurt
 ½ cup refrigerated or frozen egg product, thawed, or 2 eggs, lightly beaten
 1 teaspoon vanilla
2¼ cups all-purpose flour
 ¼ cup snipped dried apricots
 ¼ cup currants
 ¼ cup chopped walnuts, toasted

1. Preheat oven to 375°F. Spread oats in a shallow baking pan. Bake about 10 minutes or until toasted, stirring once. Lightly coat cookie sheet with cooking spray or line with parchment paper.

2. In a large bowl beat butter with a mixer on medium to high for 30 seconds. Add the next four ingredients (through allspice); beat until combined. Beat in the next three ingredients (through vanilla), scraping bowl as needed. Beat in flour. Stir in the remaining ingredients. Drop dough by teaspoons 2 inches apart onto prepared cookie sheet. Bake 9 to 11 minutes or until edges and bottoms are browned. Remove; cool on wire racks.

TO STORE: Layer cookies between sheets of waxed paper in an airtight container; cover. Store at room temperature up to 3 days or freeze up to 2 months.

Per Serving: 101 cal., 3 g fat (1 g sat. fat), 5 mg chol., 55 mg sodium, 17 g carb., 8 g sugars, 1 g fiber, 2 g pro.

PERFECT PAIR   What's better with a cookie than a glass of cold fat-free milk?

apricot-rosemary streusel bars

Prep: 40 minutes   Bake: 40 minutes at 350°F   Makes 32 servings (1 bar each)

	Nonstick cooking spray
3	cups all-purpose flour
1	cup granulated sugar
2	teaspoons snipped fresh rosemary
1	teaspoon baking powder
1	teaspoon salt
1	cup cold butter, cut up
2	15-ounce cans unpeeled apricot halves in light syrup
¾	cup granulated sugar
2	tablespoons cornstarch
⅓	cup water
2	tablespoons butter
¼	teaspoon salt
⅓	cup pine nuts
1	cup powdered sugar
¼	teaspoon vanilla
1	to 2 tablespoons milk

SIMPLE SWAP

Coarsely chop blanched almonds or hazelnuts and use them in place of the pine nuts.

1. Preheat oven to 350°F. Line a 13×9-inch baking pan with foil, extending foil over edges of the pan. Coat foil with cooking spray.

2. For crust, in a bowl stir together the next five ingredients (through 1 teaspoon salt). Using a pastry blender, cut in the 1 cup butter until mixture resembles coarse crumbs. Reserve 1½ cups of the flour mixture. Press the remaining flour mixture into the bottom of the prepared pan. Bake 10 to 12 minutes or until set.

3. Meanwhile, drain apricots, reserving ¼ cup of the liquid. In a medium saucepan combine the reserved liquid, the drained apricots, and the next five ingredients (through ¼ teaspoon salt). Cook and stir over medium heat until thick and bubbly; cook and stir 1 minute more. Spoon apricot mixture over crust in pan. Combine reserved flour mixture and the pine nuts; sprinkle over apricot mixture. Bake about 30 minutes or until bubbly around edges and topping is light brown. Cool in pan on a wire rack.

4. For icing, stir together the remaining ingredients. Stir in additional milk, 1 teaspoon at a time, to make drizzling consistency. Drizzle over uncut bars. Let stand until set. Use foil to lift uncut bars out of pan. Cut into bars.

TO STORE: Place bars in a single layer in an airtight container; cover. Store in the refrigerator up to 3 days or freeze up to 3 months.

Per Serving: 181 cal., 7 g fat (4 g sat. fat), 17 mg chol., 165 mg sodium, 28 g carb., 18 g sugars, 1 g fiber, 2 g pro.

☐ GLUTEN-FREE ☑ MAKE-AHEAD ☐ HIGH-FIBER ☐ 30-MINUTE ☑ VEGETARIAN

fresh apple bars

Prep: 20 minutes   Bake: 20 minutes at 350°F   Makes 15 servings (1 bar each)

Nonstick cooking spray
¾ cup granulated sugar
1¼ cups white whole wheat flour
1 teaspoon ground cinnamon
½ teaspoon baking soda
¼ teaspoon salt
3 tablespoons canola oil
2 eggs, lightly beaten
1 teaspoon vanilla
2 cups chopped apples
2 tablespoons white whole wheat flour
2 tablespoons packed brown sugar
1 teaspoon ground cinnamon
2 tablespoons butter

SIMPLE SWAP

All-purpose flour works the same as white whole wheat flour in this recipe.

1. Preheat oven to 350°F. Line a 13×9-inch baking pan with foil, extending foil over edges of the pan. Coat foil with cooking spray.

2. In a bowl whisk together the next five ingredients (through salt). In another bowl whisk together the next three ingredients (through vanilla); stir in apples. Add egg mixture to flour mixture; stir until combined (batter will be very stiff and doughlike). Spread batter in the prepared pan; if necessary, use slightly moistened hands to pat batter into an even layer.

3. In a medium bowl stir together the next three ingredients (through cinnamon). Using a pastry blender, cut in butter until mixture is crumbly. Sprinkle over the batter in pan. Bake about 20 minutes or until a toothpick inserted near the center comes out clean. Cool in pan on a wire rack. Use foil to lift uncut bars out of pan. Cut into bars.

TO STORE: Layer bars between sheets of waxed paper in an airtight container; cover. Store in the refrigerator up to 3 days.

Per Serving: *123 cal., 3 g fat (1 g sat. fat), 29 mg chol., 105 mg sodium, 22 g carb., 14 g sugars, 1 g fiber, 2 g pro.*

strawberry "margarita" cheesecake minis

Prep: 45 minutes   Bake: 20 minutes at 325°F   Cool: 10 minutes   Chill: 4 hours
Makes 18 servings (2 mini cheesecakes each)

1	recipe Salted Pretzel Crust
1	lime
1½	8-ounce tubs cream cheese spread, softened
½	cup sugar
1	tablespoon all-purpose flour
1	teaspoon vanilla
1	egg
1	cup sliced small strawberries
1	tablespoon sugar

SIMPLE SWAP

Any small berries, such as raspberries or blueberries, would be a fun switch for strawberries.

1. Preheat oven to 325°F. Line thirty-six 1¾-inch muffin cups with paper bake cups; set aside. Prepare Salted Pretzel Crust. Press about 1½ teaspoons pretzel mixture onto the bottom and up the sides of each prepared muffin cup. Bake 5 minutes.

2. Meanwhile, remove 1½ teaspoons lime zest and squeeze 1 tablespoon juice from lime. In a bowl beat cream cheese with a mixer on medium until smooth. Add the lime zest and next three ingredients (through vanilla). Beat until combined, scraping bowl as needed. Beat in egg on low just until combined.

3. Spoon cream cheese mixture into partially baked crusts, filling each three-fourths full. Bake 15 to 17 minutes more or until filling is set. Cool in muffin cups on wire racks 10 minutes. Remove; cool completely on wire racks. Place cooled cheesecakes in an airtight container. Cover and chill 4 to 24 hours.

4. Combine lime juice, strawberries, and the 1 tablespoon sugar. Spoon onto mini cheesecakes. If desired, sprinkle with additional lime zest.

SALTED PRETZEL CRUST: Place 1¾ cups pretzel sticks in a resealable plastic bag; seal bag. Using a rolling pin, crush pretzels to fine crumbs (you should have 1 cup). Stir together crushed pretzels, ¼ cup melted butter, and 2 tablespoons sugar.

Per Serving: 127 cal., 7 g fat (4 g sat. fat), 29 mg chol., 197 mg sodium, 14 g carb., 9 g sugars, 0 g fiber, 2 g pro.

dark chocolate mint bites

Prep: 30 minutes   Chill: 15 minutes + 1 hour   Makes: 24 servings (1 bar each)

Nonstick cooking spray
1   cup quick-cooking rolled oats
½   cup dark or semisweet chocolate pieces
6   tablespoons unsalted butter
1   cup finely crushed chocolate wafers (about 19 wafers)
1   tablespoon unsweetened cocoa powder
1   tablespoon fat-free milk
¼   teaspoon salt
½   teaspoon shortening
¾   cup powdered sugar
2   ounces reduced-fat cream cheese (Neufchâtel), softened
½   teaspoon peppermint extract
    Crushed striped round peppermint candies (optional)

SIMPLE SWAP

Little ones in the house? If you have bear-shape chocolate graham snack cookies on hand, use them in place of the chocolate wafers. About 1½ cups of bears should be enough.

1. Line an 8-inch square baking pan with foil, extending foil over the edges of the pan. Spray foil with cooking spray.

2. For crust, place oats in a food processor; cover and pulse until finely ground. In a medium saucepan combine ¼ cup of the chocolate pieces and the butter; heat and stir over low heat until melted. Stir in the oats and the next four ingredients (through salt). Press oat mixture into the prepared pan. Chill 15 minutes.

3. In the same saucepan combine remaining ¼ cup chocolate pieces and the shortening. Heat and stir over low heat until melted. In a bowl stir together powdered sugar, cream cheese, and peppermint extract until smooth. Spread over crust. Drizzle with the melted chocolate mixture.

4. Chill about 1 hour or until chocolate drizzle is set (cream cheese layer will remain soft). Using edges of foil, lift uncut bars out of the pan. If desired, sprinkle with crushed candies. Cut into 24 bars.

TO STORE: Place bars in a single layer in an airtight container; cover. Store in the refrigerator up to 3 days.

Per serving: *105 cal., 5 g fat (3 g sat. fat), 6 mg chol., 58 mg sodium, 14 g carb., 9 g sugars, 1 g fiber, 1 g pro.*

raspberry cheesecake swirl brownies

Prep: 25 minutes   Bake: 30 minutes at 350°F; 20 minutes at 325°F   Chill: 2 hours
Makes: 12 servings (1 brownie each)

Nonstick cooking spray
½   cup all-purpose flour
½   cup sugar
½   cup unsweetened cocoa powder
¼   teaspoon kosher salt
¼   teaspoon baking soda
½   cup plain fat-free Greek yogurt
1   egg
3   tablespoons fat-free milk
1   teaspoon vanilla
1   8-ounce package reduced-fat cream cheese (Neufchâtel), softened
1   cup plain fat-free Greek yogurt
2   eggs
½   cup sugar
1   teaspoon vanilla
½   cup sugar-free red raspberry preserves

SIMPLE SWAP

These versatile brownies can undergo a flavor change by using another kind of preserves. Choose apricot, blueberry, or strawberry preserves.

1. Preheat oven to 350°F. Coat an 8-inch square baking pan with cooking spray.

2. For brownie layer, in a bowl stir together the next five ingredients (through baking soda). In another bowl whisk together the next four ingredients (through vanilla). Gently fold yogurt mixture into flour mixture just until combined. Spread batter in the prepared pan.

3. For cheesecake layer, in a bowl whisk together the next five ingredients (through vanilla) until well mixed. Pour over brownie layer.

4. Drop spoonfuls of raspberry preserves onto the cheesecake layer. Using a knife or thin metal spatula, swirl the preserves into the cheesecake layer.

5. Bake 30 minutes. Reduce heat to 325°F. Bake about 20 minutes more or until cheesecake layer is set (center should not jiggle). Cool in pan on a wire rack. Cover and chill at least 2 hours before serving. Cut into 12 brownies.

TO STORE: Place bars in a single layer in an airtight container; cover. Store in the refrigerator up to 3 days.

Per serving: *183 cal., 6 g fat (3 g sat. fat), 60 mg chol., 179 mg sodium, 28 g carb., 19 g sugars, 1 g fiber, 7 g pro.*

menus

WEEK 1

	Breakfast	Lunch	Dinner
DAY 1	Farro Cereal with Pears, Walnuts, and Cherries (p. 115). 394 calories	Chicken Soup with Chive Dumplings (p. 147). 337 calories	Spicy Pork Sandwiches with Grilled Peach Chutney (p. 210) with ½ cup steamed cauliflower. 458 calories
DAY 2	2 poached eggs, 2 pieces whole wheat toast, 2 Tbsp. peanut butter, ½ apple. 534 calories	Pho-Flavor Flank Steak Lettuce Wraps (p. 45). 158 calories	Honey Mustard Salmon with Mango Quinoa (p. 234). 463 calories
DAY 3	Spicy Apple Crepes with Maple Cream (p. 193). 467 calories	2 oz. canned tuna in water, 2 Tbsp. light mayonnaise, 6 woven wheat crackers, 1 cup celery/carrot sticks. 326 calories	Balsamic Onion and Steak Pasta (p. 201). 426 calories
DAY 4	1 cup round toasted multigrain cereal, ¾ cup low-fat milk, 1 banana. 369 calories	Tofu Stir-Fry with Soba Noodles (p. 95). 300 calories	Curried Turkey and Couscous Pie (p. 229), 1 orange. 486 calories
DAY 5	Cheddar-Bacon Waffles (p. 108). 369 calories	Pork and Poblano Stew (p. 54). 300 calories	Chicken Rolls Diablo (p. 218). 453 calories
DAY 6	1 whole wheat English muffin, 1 egg, 1 oz. Candian bacon, 1 slice cheddar cheese, 8 oz. low-fat milk. 409 calories	Massaged Kale and Pork Salad (p. 214). 456 calories	Spanish Cod and Orzo Packets (p. 237). 417 calories
DAY 7	Overnight Oatmeal with Figs and Yogurt (p. 37), 6 oz. grapefruit juice. 334 calories	Roasted Vegetable Flatbreads (p. 94). 300 calories	Chicken Thighs with Gnocchi Dumplings (p. 226). 435 calories

English muffin, egg, Canadian bacon, and cheddar cheese sandwich

Farro Cereal with Pears, Walnuts, and Cherries, page 115

Blueberry-Lemon Shortcakes, page 281

Snack or Dessert	Total Calories	Today's Bonus Nutrients	To reach approx 1,600 calories add:
Italian Parmesan Pretzels (p. 257). 141 calories	1,330	Sodium count for the day is only 1,882 mg.	**Breakfast:** 6 oz. orange juice, 1 kiwifruit **Lunch:** 1 cup romaine lettuce, ¼ cup cucumber, 2 Tbsp. red onion slices, 1 Tbsp. light caesar dressing **Dinner:** 5 oz. baked sweet potato
Cherry Almond Snack Mix (p. 246). 198 calories	1,353	Enjoy 109% of the the daily value (DV) of vitamin C today.	**Breakfast:** 1 cup low-fat milk **Lunch:** 2 Tbsp. chopped peanuts **Dinner:** 1 cup sautéed zucchini and yellow peppers
½ cup low-fat cottage cheese, 1 cup raspberries. 155 calories	1,374	It's a great day for vitamin A! You get 333% of your daily value.	**Breakfast:** 1 cup grapes **Lunch:** 1 cup unsweetened vanilla almond milk **Dinner:** 1 cup spinach and 5 grape tomatoes tossed with 2 tsp. light Italian vinaigrette
Blueberry-Lemon Shortcakes (p. 281). 199 calories	1,354	Vitamin C is off the charts today! Get 411% of your daily value.	**Breakfast:** 1 slice whole wheat toast plus 1 Tbsp. apple butter **Dinner:** 1 cup steamed broccoli
½ cup frozen yogurt, ¼ cup strawberries. 223 calories	1,345	Today's plan gets you your B vitamins: 133% DV niacin and 106% DV vitamin B6.	**Breakfast:** 1 scrambled egg, ½ cup blackberries **Lunch:** 1 oz. whole grain tortilla chips **Dinner:** 1 cup steamed asparagus
Parmesan Dip (p. 254). 47 calories	1,329	Build bones with 103% DV calcium.	**Breakfast:** 6 oz. low-fat Greek yogurt **Lunch:** 1 small crusty whole wheat roll, 1 tsp. butter **Dinner:** ¾ cup steamed green beans
Silky Chocolate Pie (p. 266). 235 calories	1,354	This day has you eating enough veggies and fruit to get 453% DV vitamin C.	**Snack:** 2 stalks celery, 2 Tbsp. peanut butter **Dinner:** 1 cup Brussels sprouts roasted in 1 tsp. olive oil

Roasted Vegetable Flatbreads, page 94

Balsamic Onion and Steak Pasta, page 201

Pork Tenderloin Sandwiches with Chimichurri Sauce, page 135

WEEK 2

	Breakfast	Lunch	Dinner
DAY 1	Confetti Hash Browns and Eggs (p. 18). 240 calories	1 whole wheat sandwich thin, 3 oz. grilled chicken breast, 2 slices tomato, 2 pieces leaf lettuce, 1 thin slice Swiss cheese, 1 tsp. Dijon-style mustard, 1 cup grapes, 1 cup low-fat milk. 543 calories	Lasagna Soup (p. 233). 415 calories
DAY 2	Squash, Bacon, and Feta Breakfast Bake (p. 26). 213 calories	Grilled Flank Steak Salad (p. 119), 2 oz. whole wheat roll. 412 calories	Skillet Pork Chops with Butter Beans, Peas, and Charred Green Onions (p. 213). 467 calories
DAY 3	1 small whole wheat bagel, 2 Tbsp. light cream cheese, ¾ cup mixed fruit, 4 oz. orange juice. 462 calories	Succotash Salad with Buttermilk-Avocado Dressing (p. 148). 345 calories	Italian Meatball Rolls (p. 155). 320 calories
DAY 4	Huevos Tacos con Queso (p. 194). 402 calories	Manhattan Clam Chowder (p. 175). 308 calories	Coconut-Curry Chicken (p. 140). 393 calories
DAY 5	1 cup oatmeal, 2 Tbsp. dried fruit, 1 Tbsp. maple syrup, ½ cup honeydew, 1 cup low-fat milk. 398 calories	Bow Tie Pesto Alfredo (p. 152). 385 calories	Pork Tenderloin Sandwiches with Chimichurri Sauce (p. 135). 343 calories
DAY 6	Brunch Baked Apples with Greek Yogurt (p. 197). 438 calories	Salad with 2 cups mixed greens; ½ cup chopped grilled chicken breast; ¼ cup cucumber; ¼ cup tomatoes; ¼ cup croutons, ¼ avocado, sliced; 2 Tbsp. light balsamic vinaigrette. 321 calories	Wild Mushroom Ravioli Skillet Lasagna (p. 238). 416 calories
DAY 7	Coconut Chia Oat Bites (p. 38), 1 cup low-fat milk, ½ cup pineapple. 437 calories	Kansas City Steak Soup (p. 123). 306 calories	Hot-Spiced Pork and Rice (p. 217). 432 calories

Huevos Tacos con Queso, page 194

Lasagna Soup, page 233

Succotash Salad with Buttermilk-Avocado Dressing, page 148

Snack or Dessert	Total Calories	Today's Bonus Nutrients	To reach approx 1,600 calories add:
Chocolate Ravioli (p. 273). 134 calories	1,332	Get a healthy dose of vitamin A (130% DV) and vitamin C (218% DV).	**Breakfast:** 1 orange **Lunch:** 1 cup heart-healthy chicken noodle soup, ½ cup baby carrots **Dinner:** salad with 1 cup kale and 2 tsp. light balsamic vinaigrette
1 oz. multigrain tortilla chips, 3 Tbsp. guacamole. 230 calories	1,322	Fill up with 24 g fiber with today's menus. Boost it even more with the suggestions *at right*.	**Breakfast:** 1 small oat bran muffin **Lunch:** ¾ cup mango **Dinner:** ⅓ cup cooked brown rice
Herbed Mixed Nuts (p. 246). 189 calories	1,316	Brighten your day with 204% DV vitamin C.	**Lunch:** 1 oz. pita chips, 1 cup blackberries **Dinner:** 1 cup cooked zucchini, 1 cup low-fat milk
1 oz. wheat crackers (Wheat Thins), 1 oz. reduced-fat cheddar cheese. 248 calories	1,351	Stay sharp with 253% DV vitamin B12 today!	**Breakfast:** ½ avocado **Lunch:** 1 apple; salad with 1 cup spinach, ¼ cup sliced fennel, ¼ cup orange sections, 2 tsp. light Italian salad dressing **Dinner:** 1 cup cooked yellow squash
Creamy Rice Pudding (p. 282). 189 calories	1,315	Thiamin (143% DV) and riboflavin (111% DV) are in the spotlight today.	**Lunch:** 1½ cups corn, 1 slice Italian bread, 1 tsp. butter **Dinner:** ½ cup potatoes and ½ cup red peppers roasted in 1 tsp. olive oil
Pear-Pecan Crisp (p. 270). 201 calories	1,376	You'll meet your daily needs for 5 servings of vegetables per day.	**Breakfast:** 2 hard-cooked eggs **Lunch:** ½ cup strawberries, 1 Tbsp. sunflower seeds **Dinner:** ½ cup steamed carrots tossed with 1 tsp. butter
Berry Yogurt Parfaits (p. 250). 129 calories	1,304	Get your ABCs: 201% DV vitamin A, 99% DV vitamin B12, 120% DV niacin, 137% DV thiamin, and 233% DV vitamin C.	**Breakfast:** 1 slice whole wheat toast, 1 Tbsp. peanut butter **Lunch:** 1 cup steamed asparagus **Dinner:** ½ cup steamed snow peas

Skillet Pork Chops with Butter Beans, Peas, and Charred Green Onions, page 213

index

metric information

The charts on this page provide a guide for converting measurements from the U.S. customary system, which is used throughout this book, to the metric system.

product differences

Most of the ingredients called for in the recipes in this book are available in most countries. However, some are known by different names. Here are some common American ingredients and their possible counterparts:

- Sugar (white) is granulated, fine granulated, or castor sugar.
- Powdered sugar is icing sugar.
- All-purpose flour is enriched, bleached or unbleached white household flour. When self-rising flour is used in place of all-purpose flour in a recipe that calls for leavening, omit the leavening agent (baking soda or baking powder) and salt.
- Light-color corn syrup is golden syrup.
- Cornstarch is cornflour.
- Baking soda is bicarbonate of soda.
- Vanilla or vanilla extract is vanilla essence.
- Green, red, or yellow sweet peppers are capsicums or bell peppers.
- Golden raisins are sultanas.

volume and weight

The United States traditionally uses cup measures for liquid and solid ingredients. The chart below shows the approximate imperial and metric equivalents. If you are accustomed to weighing solid ingredients, the following approximate equivalents will be helpful.

- 1 cup butter, castor sugar, or rice = 8 ounces = ½ pound = 250 grams
- 1 cup flour = 4 ounces = ¼ pound = 125 grams
- 1 cup icing sugar = 5 ounces = 150 grams

Canadian and U.S. volume for a cup measure is 8 fluid ounces (237 ml), but the standard metric equivalent is 250 ml.

1 British imperial cup is 10 fluid ounces.

In Australia, 1 tablespoon equals 20 ml, and there are 4 teaspoons in the Australian tablespoon.

Spoon measures are used for smaller amounts of ingredients. Although the size of the tablespoon varies slightly in different countries, for practical purposes and for recipes in this book, a straight substitution is all that's necessary. Measurements made using cups or spoons always should be level unless stated otherwise.

common weight range replacements

Imperial / U.S.	Metric
½ ounce	15 g
1 ounce	25 g or 30 g
4 ounces (¼ pound)	115 g or 125 g
8 ounces (½ pound)	225 g or 250 g
16 ounces (1 pound)	450 g or 500 g
1¼ pounds	625 g
1½ pounds	750 g
2 pounds or 2¼ pounds	1,000 g or 1 Kg

oven temperature equivalents

Fahrenheit Setting	Celsius Setting*	Gas Setting
300°F	150°C	Gas Mark 2 (very low)
325°F	160°C	Gas Mark 3 (low)
350°F	180°C	Gas Mark 4 (moderate)
375°F	190°C	Gas Mark 5 (moderate)
400°F	200°C	Gas Mark 6 (hot)
425°F	220°C	Gas Mark 7 (hot)
450°F	230°C	Gas Mark 8 (very hot)
475°F	240°C	Gas Mark 9 (very hot)
500°F	260°C	Gas Mark 10 (extremely hot)
Broil	Broil	Grill

*Electric and gas ovens may be calibrated using celsius. However, for an electric oven, increase celsius setting 10 to 20 degrees when cooking above 160°C. For convection or forced air ovens (gas or electric), lower the temperature setting 25°F/10°C when cooking at all heat levels.

baking pan sizes

Imperial / U.S.	Metric
9×1½-inch round cake pan	22- or 23×4-cm (1.5 L)
9×1½-inch pie plate	22- or 23×4-cm (1 L)
8×8×2-inch square cake pan	20×5-cm (2 L)
9×9×2-inch square cake pan	22- or 23×4.5-cm (2.5 L)
11×7×1½-inch baking pan	28×17×4-cm (2 L)
2-quart rectangular baking pan	30×19×4.5-cm (3 L)
13×9×2-inch baking pan	34×22×4.5-cm (3.5 L)
15×10×1-inch jelly roll pan	40×25×2-cm
9×5×3-inch loaf pan	23×13×8-cm (2 L)
2-quart casserole	2 L

U.S. / standard metric equivalents

⅛ teaspoon = 0.5 ml	
¼ teaspoon = 1 ml	
½ teaspoon = 2 ml	
1 teaspoon = 5 ml	
1 tablespoon = 15 ml	
2 tablespoons = 25 ml	
¼ cup = 2 fluid ounces = 50 ml	
⅓ cup = 3 fluid ounces = 75 ml	
½ cup = 4 fluid ounces = 125 ml	
⅔ cup = 5 fluid ounces = 150 ml	
¾ cup = 6 fluid ounces = 175 ml	
1 cup = 8 fluid ounces = 250 ml	
2 cups = 1 pint = 500 ml	
1 quart = 1 litre	